THE CHASE
QUIZBOOK

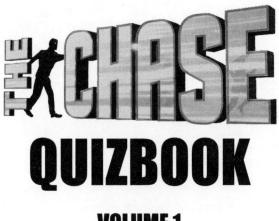

QUIZBOOK

VOLUME 1

Foreword by Bradley Walsh

**An all new quizbook with
ITV's most popular teatime show**

An Hachette UK Company
www.hachette.co.uk

First published in Great Britain in 2015 by Hamlyn,
a division of Octopus Publishing Group Ltd
Carmelite House
50 Victoria Embankment
London EC4Y 0DZ
www.octopusbooks.co.uk

ISBN 978-0-600-63280-1

A CIP catalogue record for this book is available from the
British Library.

Printed and bound in the UK.

10 9 8 7 6 5 4 3 2

Contents

FOREWORD

I remember the very day that, for me, *The Chase* was born.

It was a sunny day in April 2009 and I was outside the ITV Network Centre when, on a whim, I telephoned the then Controller of ITV Daytime and Factual, Alison Sharman. 'Have you got five minutes for a cuppa and chat?' I asked. 'Yes, pop up' came the reply. I had no idea that the cuppa and chat was to be so important and life changing for so many people.

Following a varied career as a footballer, stand-up comedian and presenter I had happily transitioned to acting. I love being an actor and ITV Drama have always supported me with different projects including *Coronation Street* (Danny Baldwin my character had been a particular favourite with Alison Sharman's mum which no doubt helped this story) and, of course, *Law & Order: UK*.

After a general chat about the business I said to Ali that, although I love drama, I wanted to 'keep my hand in' with light entertainment. Straight away Ali rang her second in command, Diane Howie, who came into the office with a single sheet of A4 paper which contained the outline of a quiz show. I studied it for a few minutes. 'What do you think?' asked Ali. 'Yeah, I like it, it could work' I said. 'Well we are going to do an office run-through in a couple of days', and before she could say anymore I said 'I'll do it for you!'

Two days later I was in a meeting room with the show's Executive Producer Michael Kelpie and his team. We did a run-through with Shaun Wallace and straight away it felt original and special.

FOREWORD

The banter was flowing, the team allowed me to take the mickey out of the Chaser when he got a question wrong, and he took it on the chin... I loved it!

We were given a pilot series of ten shows filmed in Manchester at the beginning of June to be shown at the end of the month on ITV1. Midway through the second week, we were getting more viewers than *The Weakest Link* on BBC1 which, up to that point, had been the highest rated quiz show on British TV. It was a big moment and the first of many for everyone concerned with *The Chase*.

Six years later, we are in the middle of filming series 9 containing an eye-watering 190 episodes! In the autumn we will be filming 16 'Celebrity Specials' which will air in prime time. *The Chase* is not only a hit here in the UK but also in the USA, Russia, Germany, Australia and Norway to name but a few.

Almost everyone I meet always asks me the same thing. 'Because you work on *The Chase* it must make you clever!' I always reply with the same answer, 'It's safer asking the questions!' although I clearly got one thing right, back in April 2009, when I casually suggested 'Yeah, it could work' and 'Yeah, I like it' but then again, I am always one for grossly understating everything!

This book is something we've wanted to do for a long time. We've tried to structure the questions so that you can enjoy the thrill of *The Chase* with your family and friends. It might inspire you to take on a Chaser and win a load of cash!

Bradley Walsh, 2015

HOW TO USE THIS BOOK

Since it launched on ITV in 2009, *The Chase* – hosted by Bradley Walsh – has become one of television's most popular quiz games. Numerous players, including celebrities, have accepted the challenge to compete against the quiz brains of its four resident Chasers: the Governess, the Beast, the Sinnerman, and the Barrister.

In this book, you and your family and friends can test your general knowledge skills against each other in the three familiar rounds from the show. As questions have been taken from broadcast editions of *The Chase*, you can even compare your scores with those of the Chasers themselves. Even they didn't always answer correctly, so see if you can do better!

There are 40 quizzes in each of the three sections, a total of 2,000 questions, with all answers at the back of the book. You can use the book to devise your own Chase quiz in any way you choose. However, we suggest the following scenarios for solo players or for groups of two or more players:

For solo play:

Round 1: In the *Cash Builder* round, the player faces 15 questions. They may award themselves a score (eg. 1,000 points) for each correct answer. When all the questions have been answered, the player's total points score forms the basis for what happens in Round 2: the *Head-to-Head Questions*.

Round 2: In the *Head-to-Head Questions*, the player faces 12 questions, with multiple-choice answers. Here they can play against the Chaser and decide on an offer depending on their score in Round 1 and how close they want to start to the Chaser: start one place closer for double points or one place further away for half the points. After completing all the questions for that round the player can use the grid on the reverse of the jacket to check their progress question by question using the answers at the back. They can see which answers the Chaser got wrong (marked with an asterisk), and work out if they outran the Chaser. If they survived then it's on to the *Final Chase*.

HOW TO USE THIS BOOK

Round 3: In the *Final Chase*, there are 23 questions to answer. Again, the player can compare his/her score with that of the Chaser by checking the answers at the back: in each game, there is a specific number of correct answers required to beat the Chaser's score.

For two or more players:

Round 1: In the *Cash Builder* round, each player faces 15 questions. They may award themselves a score (eg. 1,000 points) for every correct answer. When all the questions have been answered, each player's total points score forms the basis for what happens in Round 2: the *Head-to-Head Questions*.

Round 2: In the *Head-to-Head Questions*, a Chaser is appointed from the group of players. Each of the other players can compete individually against the Chaser in a round of 12 questions, each with three multiple-choice answers.

Before play begins in this round, the Chaser can offer each player one of three challenges: either they can stick with their Round 1 score, or alternatively accept a higher or lower offer of the Chaser's choice.

In this round, both player and Chaser can track their progress with counters on the specially designed grid displayed on the reverse of the jacket. If the player reaches the finish line first, they win. But if the Chaser reaches the agreed number of correct answers and crosses the line before the player, then the player has been 'caught' by the Chaser, and is out of the game.

If there are multiple players competing against the Chaser, whoever has not been eliminated can take part in the *Final Chase* round.

Round 3: In the *Final Chase*, the remaining player or players face(s) 23 questions before the Chaser faces a different set to see if they can catch and overtake the other player(s) and win the game. Alternatively, the Chaser and the players can compete on the same set of questions – whoever 'buzzes in' or answers first with the correct answer wins the point. If there is more than one player taking part against the Chaser, whoever scores the most points is the winner.

GOOD LUCK AND ENJOY THE CHASE!

CASH BUILDER
QUESTIONS

Cash Builder Quiz 1

1/1 ▶ Which TV network owns digital channels 4Seven and More4?

1/2 ▶ The song 'Take A Chance on Me' features in what stage musical?

1/3 ▶ Which British tennis player won the 1972 Australian Open ladies' singles title?

1/4 ▶ A common addition to the words on a 'kiss me quick' hat is 'squeeze me...' what?

1/5 ▶ The Archbishop of Buenos Aires took up what position in 2013?

1/6 ▶ Coleridge's 'Rime of the Ancient Mariner' first appeared in what book of poems?

1/7 ▶ What party did Winston Churchill rejoin in the 1920s?

CASH BUILDER QUESTIONS

1/8 ▶ What former home of the Earl of Shrewsbury is a Staffordshire amusement park?

1/9 ▶ The play *Black Coffee* featured what Agatha Christie detective?

1/10 ▶ Which TOWIE star presented *Party Wright Around the World* on ITV2?

1/11 ▶ What word for a camera image comes from the Greek for 'light' and 'draw'?

1/12 ▶ Which P G Wodehouse character belonged to the Junior Ganymede Club for valets?

1/13 ▶ The 1921 Treaty of Ankara was between France and what other country?

1/14 ▶ Since 1979 the US have competed against what team for the Ryder Cup?

1/15 ▶ Sleeping Beauty Castle is an attraction at what California theme park?

Cash Builder Quiz 2

2/1 ▶ Traditionally, what cards are sent anonymously on 14 February?

2/2 ▶ What Australian soap first appeared on UK TV in October 1986?

2/3 ▶ What married name did Argentine-born politician Eva Duarte take in 1945?

2/4 ▶ Which tall footballer is famed for his celebratory 'robot' dance?

2/5 ▶ The name of what planet begins with two vowels?

2/6 ▶ In what opera is a girl nearly executed for a crime committed by a bird?

2/7 ▶ Which Canadian pop star is the subject of the 3D documentary film *Believe*?

2/8 ▶ King Edward the First bestowed what title on his son in 1301?

2/9 ▶ Reverend Elijah Craig is credited with inventing what type of US whiskey?

2/10 ▶ Founded in 1975, what company's name combines the words 'microcomputer' and 'software'?

2/11 ▶ Which girl band from *The X Factor* released the 2013 single 'Move'?

2/12 ▶ What is the capital city of Lithuania?

2/13 ▶ What company makes Milk Tray and Roses chocolates?

QUIZ 1–2

2/14 ▶ Which acting dame plays the title role in the 2013 film *Philomena*?

2/15 ▶ What West End theatre shares its name and location with a hotel?

Cash Builder Quiz 3

3/1 ▶ 'St Martin's Summer' is a name for warm weather in what other season?

3/2 ▶ Spencer Matthews is a star of what 'constructed reality' TV show?

3/3 ▶ In 1889, what replaced the Washington Monument as the world's tallest structure?

3/4 ▶ Who was the first Labour party leader to win three successive general elections?

3/5 ▶ With which king is the saying 'Divorced, beheaded, died' associated?

CASH BUILDER QUESTIONS

3/6 ▶ In the game 'Rock Paper Scissors', what beats 'Scissors'?

3/7 ▶ What 2012 Nicki Minaj song shares its title with a Renault car catchphrase?

3/8 ▶ In maths, simultaneous and quadratic are examples of what?

3/9 ▶ Diego is the sabre-toothed tiger in what animated film series?

3/10 ▶ At the 1994 World Cup, which Brazilian striker won the Golden Ball award?

3/11 ▶ Herbology and divination are subjects studied at what fictional school?

3/12 ▶ The 19th-century Peninsular War refers to what peninsula?

3/13 ▶ Who won *Celebrity Big Brother* in 2006 after pretending to be a celebrity?

3/14 ▶ What landlocked lake in the Middle East is also called the 'Salt Sea'?

3/15 ▶ Something uncomplicated is said to be as easy as falling off what?

Cash Builder Quiz 4

4/1 ▶ What name links both a lamb-owning and a 'contrary' nursery rhyme character?

4/2 ▶ 'She's into superstitions' are the opening words of what Ricky Martin hit?

4/3 ▶ What London stadium is the world's largest venue dedicated to rugby union?

4/4 ▶ For corporation tax, the 'financial year' starts on the first of what month?

CASH BUILDER QUESTIONS

4/5 ▶ Which Italian tenor was the first artist to sell 1 million records?

4/6 ▶ Which TV teenagers 'morphed' into kung-fu superheroes to fight evil aliens?

4/7 ▶ The Emperor Augustus was the great-nephew and heir of which Roman?

4/8 ▶ What fabric is made from the same plant that produces linseed oil?

4/9 ▶ A lion and what mythical creature appear on the Royal Arms?

4/10 ▶ Who was the first title character in a Disney film to be based on a real person?

4/11 ▶ The frequently asked rhetorical question is 'how long is a piece of...' what?

QUIZ 3–4

4/12 ▶ 'Advice from a Caterpillar' is the fifth chapter of what Lewis Carroll book?

4/13 ▶ What Daft Punk song won 'Record of the Year' at the 2014 Grammy Awards?

4/14 ▶ 'If You Tolerate This Your Children Will Be Next' was a hit for what Welsh band?

4/15 ▶ The Sea of Crises and the crater Kepler are on what celestial body?

Cash Builder Quiz 5

5/1 ▶ In the Harry Potter series, which wizarding family lives in The Burrow?

5/2 ▶ What country do you reach first if you sail due south from the Isle of Wight?

5/3 ▶ Frankie Muniz played a child genius in what American sitcom?

CASH BUILDER QUESTIONS

5/4 ▷ Scott Waites won the BDO World Championship in what sport in 2013?

5/5 ▷ Which TV chefs travelled around on motorcycles for their show *Bakeation*?

5/6 ▷ Which King was victorious at the 1513 Battle of The Spurs?

5/7 ▷ To have an unyielding approach is to 'rule with an iron...' what?

5/8 ▷ When the American vice president flies on an aeroplane it has what call sign?

5/9 ▷ The 2013 TV superhero series is entitled *Marvel's Agents of...* what?

5/10 ▷ The name of what style of entertainment derives from the Italian for 'little dance'?

5/11 ▶ On a traditional Cluedo board the name of what room begins with a 'D'?

5/12 ▶ What Jonathan Larson musical was inspired by Puccini's opera *La Bohème*?

5/13 ▶ The slogan 'Your King and Country need you' was coined for what conflict?

5/14 ▶ Anne Bonney and Mary Read were both infamous female what?

5/15 ▶ 'I'm a model you know what I mean' is a line from what Right Said Fred hit?

Cash Builder Quiz 6

6/1 ▶ Two of what animal appeared on the original cover of *Watership Down*?

6/2 ▶ What primary colour is the 'Little Miss' character Little Miss Sunshine?

CASH BUILDER QUESTIONS

6/3 ▷ Only honey bees of what gender can sting?

6/4 ▷ At what country estate was the German Enigma code broken in World War Two?

6/5 ▷ In 2013, Laure Prouvost won what major UK art prize?

6/6 ▷ Which TV chef presented the Channel Four show *Fantastical Food*?

6/7 ▷ What Lloyd Webber musical features the song 'Light At The End Of The Tunnel'?

6/8 ▷ A uniformed member of what emergency service is on the Neighbourhood Watch logo?

6/9 ▷ The capital of British Columbia is named after which British monarch?

6/10 ▶ Which weekday Radio 2 DJ also hosts a
Sunday Love Songs show?

6/11 ▶ A memory aid for changing the clocks is
'Spring forward,' what '... back'?

6/12 ▶ In 2000, which Tsar of Russia was made a saint
by the Orthodox church?

6/13 ▶ If you are determined or stand firm you are said
to 'grit your...' what?

6/14 ▶ The Staten Island ferry links Staten Island to what
New York borough?

6/15 ▶ Which talent show judge features on Dizzee
Rascal's single 'Something Really Bad'?

Cash Builder Quiz 7

7/1 ▶ What Swedish company's Lövet table was its first
flat-pack furniture product?

CASH BUILDER QUESTIONS

7/2 ▶ John Profumo resigned as an MP for what party in 1963?

7/3 ▶ Which famous Italian artist died in the Loire valley in 1519?

7/4 ▶ The calcium carbonate residue that forms in a kettle is better known as what?

7/5 ▶ In what decade did Bobby Moore make his debut for Fulham?

7/6 ▶ Elliott and his dog Harvey appear in what 1982 Spielberg film?

7/7 ▶ Which former midwife wrote the memoir *Farewell to the East End*?

7/8 ▶ What was the profession of Tom Hanks's character in the film *Apollo 13*?

7/9 ▶ Bill Bowerman co-founded the company that became what US sportswear giant?

7/10 ▶ Which detective refers to the character Irene Adler as 'The Woman'?

7/11 ▶ Which of the armed forces used the term 'milk run' for wartime missions?

7/12 ▶ Which character from *Winnie-the-Pooh* could be described as a 'swine'?

7/13 ▶ In Manhattan, the neighbourhood known as NoHo stands for 'North of...' what street?

7/14 ▶ Who took his stage name from bandmates John Baldry and Elton Dean?

7/15 ▶ An equine statue by Elisabeth Frink and a novel by Michael Morpurgo share what name?

Cash Builder Quiz 8

8/1 ▶ How many throwing events are there in an Olympic men's decathlon?

8/2 ▶ The party game involving a search for a sewing aid is 'Hunt the...' what?

8/3 ▶ Which writer and comedienne released a fitness DVD called *Maracattack*?

8/4 ▶ What apple variety shares its name with a girl gang member in the musical *Grease*?

8/5 ▶ What jeweller uses a distinctive blue box and white ribbon packaging?

8/6 ▶ In another name change, which rapper has begun calling himself 'Snoopzilla'?

8/7 ▶ *The Umbrellas* is an 1880s' painting by which French Impressionist?

QUIZ 7–8

8/8 ▶ Pleasure Beach and Tower are stops on what town's tram system?

8/9 ▶ Which former Disney star released the 2013 album *Bangerz*?

8/10 ▶ Lorenzo the Magnificent was a member of what Florentine family?

8/11 ▶ The ship *Mi Amigo* sank in 1980 while carrying what pirate radio station?

8/12 ▶ What animal traditionally provides children's rides on the beach?

8/13 ▶ What colour was the famous track suit worn by Uma Thurman in *Kill Bill*?

8/14 ▶ Who was the Roman equivalent of the Greek god Eros?

8/15 ▶ The title of what satirical magazine means a hired detective?

Cash Builder Quiz 9

9/1 ▶ In 2013 who was the first professional golfer to do *Strictly Come Dancing*?

9/2 ▶ What river acts as a border between Switzerland and Liechtenstein?

9/3 ▶ The Final of what football competition was first held in 1872?

9/4 ▶ What total is reached if you add Enid Blyton's Famous group to her Secret group?

9/5 ▶ Who played Nick Fury in *Iron Man 2*, *Captain America* and *Avengers Assemble*?

9/6 ▶ What meat product often features in a Punch and Judy show?

QUIZ 8–9

9/7 ▶ Bowser, the king of the Koopas, is an arch-enemy in what Nintendo series?

9/8 ▶ If someone catches you committing a crime you have been 'caught red...' what?

9/9 ▶ Which Frenchman composed *Bolero* as a ballet score?

9/10 ▶ Ashton Kutcher played what entrepreneur in the film *Jobs*?

9/11 ▶ A reorganisation of senior political ministers is called a 'Cabinet...' what?

9/12 ▶ Which former Pussycat Doll created a clothing range for online store Missguided?

9/13 ▶ What was the name of the fictional author of *Fly Fishing* in Yellow Pages adverts?

9/14 ▶ Which religious man was *TIME* magazine's Person of the Year for 2013?

9/15 ▶ Woody Harrelson plays cop Martin Hart in what Louisiana-set TV crime series?

Cash Builder Quiz 10

10/1 ▶ In what southern English county is the seaside resort of Selsey?

10/2 ▶ The book *Oswald's Tale* by Norman Mailer is about which assassin?

10/3 ▶ At the start of a snooker frame, what ball is placed between yellow and green?

10/4 ▶ The music hall song 'Daisy Bell' has the famous line: 'A bicycle built for...' how many?

10/5 ▶ The title character of what Japanese arcade game eats 'power pellets'?

QUIZ 9-10

10/6 ▶ Ving Rhames played Marsellus Wallace in what Tarantino film?

10/7 ▶ Which controversial Scottish politician is nicknamed 'Gorgeous George'?

10/8 ▶ In *The Jungle Book* Messua believes who is her long-lost son?

10/9 ▶ Which veteran comedian stars in the radio show *When the Dog Dies*?

10/10 ▶ Events taking place in quick succession are said to come 'thick and...' what?

10/11 ▶ In 2014, Cate Blanchett won a Golden Globe for her role in what Woody Allen film?

10/12 ▶ Which god of wine features with Ariadne in the title of a Titian painting?

10/13 ▶ In telegrams, the word 'STOP' replaced what punctuation mark?

10/14 ▶ Who recorded the 2013 Children in Need single 'How Long Will I Love You'?

10/15 ▶ Louis the Twelfth of France married the sister of which Tudor king?

Cash Builder Quiz 11

11/1 ▶ Which writer's railway series included the book *Tank Engine Thomas Again*?

11/2 ▶ Found on the Falklands, the Magellanic and gentoo are species of what flightless bird?

11/3 ▶ In the name of the company BAE Systems, the 'BAE' stands for what?

11/4 ▶ Which future Prime Minister became Secretary of War in 1919?

11/5 ▶ Sam Worthington played a disabled ex-marine in what sci-fi film?

11/6 ▶ What Queensland city is named after the Governor of New South Wales in the 1820s?

11/7 ▶ 'Uncle Ned' is cockney rhyming slang for what part of the body?

11/8 ▶ *Love in the Future* was a 2013 album by which American singer-songwriter?

11/9 ▶ What 1993 Irvine Welsh novel is set mostly in Edinburgh?

11/10 ▶ Asteroid 3-3-2-5 is named after what spacecraft from *Doctor Who*?

11/11 ▶ Which chef opened his Rhodes in the Square restaurant in 1998?

11/12 ▶ Directed by Karl Lagerfeld, *Once Upon a Time* is a short film about what fashion house?

11/13 ▶ What is the only county of the Irish Republic beginning with the letter 'G'?

11/14 ▶ Which veteran singer has released five volumes of his *Great American Songbook*?

11/15 ▶ What bird does Shakespeare call the 'bird of night' in *Julius Caesar*?

Cash Builder Quiz 12

12/1 ▶ If you serve someone well you are said to wait on them 'hand and...' what?

12/2 ▶ The Frank McCourt memoir *Angela's Ashes* is set in the US and what other country?

12/3 ▶ What 2013 film stars Maggie Smith as Jean, a new arrival at a home for retired musicians?

12/4 ▷ King John's Great Seal was attached to what document in a meadow in Runnymede?

12/5 ▷ What's the term for a plot of rented land used for growing vegetables or flowers?

12/6 ▷ A crown is the logo of what luxury watch company founded in 1905?

12/7 ▷ In the UK, what is the highest number used in a standard bingo game?

12/8 ▷ Which singer became the oldest-ever BRIT award winner in 2014?

12/9 ▷ 'Ahab's Leg' and 'The Honor and Glory of Whaling' are chapters in what novel?

12/10 ▷ The glue on what country's postage stamps is certified kosher?

CASH BUILDER QUESTIONS

12/11 ▶ In what decade was the first *Guinness Book of Records* released in the UK?

12/12 ▶ 'How I wonder what you are' is the second line of what nursery rhyme?

12/13 ▶ What Finnish company launched the XL smartphone in 2014?

12/14 ▶ Which Canadian rapper shares his name with an Elizabethan naval hero?

12/15 ▶ An orrery shows the movements of the planets around what heavenly body?

Cash Builder Quiz 13

13/1 ▶ What group of superheroes features in the 2014 film *Days of Future Past*?

13/2 ▶ Members of the Royal Family are baptised with water from what Biblical river?

13/3 ▶ In 2013, which world leader had the most followers on Twitter?

13/4 ▶ Pleather is a synthetic fabric named after leather and what other material?

13/5 ▶ In 2013, Kaká rejoined which Italian football team from Real Madrid?

13/6 ▶ The catchphrase used by Andy Millman in *Extras* is 'Are you having a...' what?

13/7 ▶ The First World War Battles of Ypres took place in what country?

13/8 ▶ *To Cut a Long Story Short* is the autobiography of which Spandau Ballet member?

13/9 ▶ The name of what orange-flavoured liqueur means 'triple dry'?

13/10 ▶ A popular myth is that so-called 'dog years' equate to how many 'human years'?

13/11 ▶ Traditionally, what *Cinderella* pantomime character shares his name with fastening devices on clothes?

13/12 ▶ Which footballer captained England at the 2006 World Cup?

13/13 ▶ 'Pocket' and 'Advance' were models of which handheld Nintendo console?

13/14 ▶ In 41 BC, which Egyptian queen was summoned to Tarsus by Mark Antony?

13/15 ▶ Julius Nyerere was the first president of which African country?

Cash Builder Quiz 14

14/1 ▶ What space agency operates the Armstrong Flight Research Center?

14/2 ▶ The full title of the Oscar-nominated film is *House of Flying...* what?

14/3 ▶ At customs, green and what other colour channel are deemed 'nothing to declare'?

14/4 ▶ A beauty spot is traditionally worn on what part of a woman's body?

14/5 ▶ According to the advertising slogan, 'the car in front is a...' what?

14/6 ▶ Which Rat Pack member had a 1950s Number One with 'Memories are Made of This'?

14/7 ▶ The US Mint's first coins were made from copper, silver and what other metal?

14/8 ▶ 'The Supreme Order of Christ' is awarded by which religious leader?

CASH BUILDER QUESTIONS

14/9 ▶ The interior angles of a trapezium add up to how many degrees?

14/10 ▶ Which late boxer won the BBC's Sports Personality of the Year award twice?

14/11 ▶ *The Lost Boy* and *A Man Named Dave* were sequels to what book?

14/12 ▶ What large reptile gets its name from the Ancient Greek word for 'lizard'?

14/13 ▶ What type of sugar is known in the US as 'confectioners' sugar'?

14/14 ▶ In *Dynasty*, which of the Colbys was played by John James?

14/15 ▶ What is the first month in the calendar year NOT to have a bank holiday?

Cash Builder Quiz 15

15/1 ▶ What word goes after 'buzz' and 'under' to give the names of two hairstyles?

15/2 ▶ In 1953, King Saud became ruler of what Middle Eastern country?

15/3 ▶ In the saying, what organ do you 'cross' when you make a pledge or promise?

15/4 ▶ The Loire is the longest river in what country?

15/5 ▶ The 2012 memoir *Joseph Anton* is which author's account of his life in hiding?

15/6 ▶ In 1978, Leon Spinks was the last man to be defeated by which legendary boxer?

15/7 ▶ Comedienne Joan Rivers once said which British rock singer had 'child-bearing lips'?

CASH BUILDER QUESTIONS

15/8 ▶ What major 1746 battle in Scotland lasted around 40 minutes?

15/9 ▶ What nickname is shared by the states of Florida and Queensland?

15/10 ▶ Which crooner sang 'Swinging on a Star' in the film *Going My Way*?

15/11 ▶ Brian Cox and Robin Ince's radio show is called 'The Infinite...' what?

15/12 ▶ 'Maoism' is a doctrine named after a Communist leader of what country?

15/13 ▶ Which swimming and cycling paralympian was made a Dame in 2012?

15/14 ▶ Marcus Andronicus is the brother of what Shakespeare title character?

QUIZ 15

15/15 ▶ Complete the line from the traditional song:
'What shall we do with the drunken…'

Cash Builder Quiz 16

16/1 ▶ Beijing's Forbidden City was built by what
Chinese dynasty?

16/2 ▶ In *Vanity Fair*, which Frenchman does Thackeray
refer to as 'the Corsican upstart'?

16/3 ▶ How many different colours are used in the regular
Google logo?

16/4 ▶ In the film *Dirty Dancing*, which actor says the line
'Nobody puts Baby in a corner'?

16/5 ▶ Harris Tweed, Extra Special Agent, first appeared
in what British comic?

16/6 ▶ Plastic bottles of semi-skimmed milk usually have
what colour caps?

CASH BUILDER QUESTIONS

16/7 ▶ What American university shares its name with a Parisian cathedral?

16/8 ▶ Which former Tory MP wrote the plays *Beyond Reasonable Doubt* and *Exclusive*?

16/9 ▶ What word links a combination of musical notes and a state of peace?

16/10 ▶ Which of the four main characters in *The Wind in the Willows* is an amphibian?

16/11 ▶ What's the capital of Hungary?

16/12 ▶ What word can mean both a bet and a flat-bottomed boat?

16/13 ▶ The Tom Cruise film *Valkyrie* is about a plot to kill which German leader?

16/14 ▶ In the Bible, two of the four gospels are named after men with what initial?

16/15 ▶ Guy Haines and Charles Bruno are conspirators in what Patricia Highsmith novel?

Cash Builder Quiz 17

17/1 ▶ Wrestler Hulk Hogan used what song by Survivor as his entrance theme?

17/2 ▶ Which Spanish surrealist painted *Swans Reflecting Elephants*?

17/3 ▶ Which singer played Motormouth Maybelle in the 2007 remake of *Hairspray*?

17/4 ▶ Due to EU protection, Retsina can be made only in Greece and what other country?

17/5 ▶ Which future President did Laura Welch marry in Midland, Texas in 1977?

CASH BUILDER QUESTIONS

17/6 ▶ Making private revelations in a tabloid newspaper is known as 'kiss and...' what?

17/7 ▶ In fashion, what is the English equivalent of the phrase 'prêt-à-porter'?

17/8 ▶ 'The road is long' are the opening words of what The Hollies hit?

17/9 ▶ The novel *Memoirs of a Geisha* is set in what country?

17/10 ▶ What type of chocolate biscuit is named after a French Royal House?

17/11 ▶ Jon Heder played the title role in what 2004 high school comedy film?

17/12 ▶ The name of what chess piece comes first alphabetically?

17/13 ▶ Which masked Wild West hero debuted on Radio WXYZ in 1933?

17/14 ▶ Katarina Johnson-Thompson broke whose British junior heptathlon record in 2012?

17/15 ▶ Someone being a bit ditsy is said to be having a what colour hair moment?

Cash Builder Quiz 18

18/1 ▶ The Irish dish 'champ' is potato mashed with what vegetable?

18/2 ▶ What song is sung during the *Sound of Music* puppet show?

18/3 ▶ The Peninsular and Oriental Steam Navigation Company is usually known by what name?

18/4 ▶ What Lionel Richie hit features the lyrics 'party, karamu, fiesta, forever'?

CASH BUILDER QUESTIONS

18/5 ▶ What's the only planet named after a god from Greek mythology?

18/6 ▶ Michael Douglas won a 2013 Emmy for playing which flamboyant pianist?

18/7 ▶ Heathrow was officially opened as a civil airport in what decade?

18/8 ▶ What's the total number of characters in a National Insurance number?

18/9 ▶ In the rhyme, what sort of shells adorn the garden of 'Mary, Mary quite contrary'?

18/10 ▶ In what film does Johnny Depp have a talent for hedge trimming and cutting hair?

18/11 ▶ What river forms the border between Texas and Mexico?

18/12 ▶ What breakfast cereal had the advertising slogan 'Tell 'em about the honey, Mummy'?

18/13 ▶ In 1877, which inventor set up the Bell Telephone Company?

18/14 ▶ In a classical concert, how many people would normally perform a cadenza?

18/15 ▶ What word links browning the skin and turning hides into leather?

Cash Builder Quiz 19

19/1 ▶ What instrument does Harry Judd play in the band McFly?

19/2 ▶ What Russian space station orbited the Earth more than 86,000 times?

19/3 ▶ What E L James novel is based on her online story 'Master of the Universe'?

CASH BUILDER QUESTIONS

19/4 ▶ What river does New York's George Washington Bridge cross?

19/5 ▶ A quiet period before a flurry of activity is 'the calm before the...' what?

19/6 ▶ *My World* was the platinum-selling debut EP by which Canadian pop star?

19/7 ▶ Ninian Park is the former ground of what football club?

19/8 ▶ In what board game has a murder victim been found on the stairs?

19/9 ▶ What Irish whiskey cream liqueur is named after a London hotel?

19/10 ▶ 'Water, water, everywhere / Nor any drop to drink' are lines by which poet?

19/11 ▶ 'LouLou' is Sharon Osbourne's nickname for which fellow judge of *The X Factor*?

19/12 ▶ The Throckmorton Plot was an attempt to remove which English Queen?

19/13 ▶ Which German supermodel was *FHM*'s first ever 'Sexiest Woman in the World'?

19/14 ▶ Michelangelo's artwork *The Creation of Adam* is on what part of the Sistine Chapel?

19/15 ▶ Who played Johnny Cash in the 2005 film *Walk the Line*?

Cash Builder Quiz 20

20/1 ▶ What is the national currency of New Zealand?

20/2 ▶ A very healthy person is said to be as fit as what insect?

CASH BUILDER QUESTIONS

20/3 ▶ In a 1995 media battle, Blur beat which band to Number One in the singles chart?

20/4 ▶ The first Formula One Grand Prix in Asia took place in what country?

20/5 ▶ A haemometer is an instrument used for testing what bodily fluid?

20/6 ▶ A spider has how many more legs than Spider-Man?

20/7 ▶ What TV series set in a Bristol school starred Andrew Lincoln?

20/8 ▶ What name is given to a cinema complex with several screens?

20/9 ▶ Which male ballet dancer was the original Mr Mistoffelees in *Cats*?

20/10 ▶ What bank did rogue trader Nick Leeson bring down?

20/11 ▶ What book and film series inspired the phrases 'Team Edward' and 'Team Jacob'?

20/12 ▶ Prince William was christened in the Music Room of what palace?

20/13 ▶ In a rhyming phrase, if you like something it 'floats your...' what?

20/14 ▶ Which royal took part in a 'Walking With the Wounded' trek across Antarctica?

20/15 ▶ Until 1996, the village of Esholt provided the exterior locations in what TV soap?

Cash Builder Quiz 21

21/1 ▶ If Christmas Eve is a Monday, what day will Boxing Day fall on?

CASH BUILDER QUESTIONS

21/2 ▶ In *The Silence of the Lambs*, Clarice Starling works for what bureau?

21/3 ▶ What chocolate bar used to be called Rowntree's Chocolate Crisp?

21/4 ▶ 'Pour myself a cup of ambition' is a line in what Dolly Parton hit?

21/5 ▶ What football governing body has its HQ in Nyon, Switzerland?

21/6 ▶ The fabric linen is made from the fibres of what plant?

21/7 ▶ What number is both the cube of four and the square of eight?

21/8 ▶ In athletics, a bar is raised in the high jump and what other event?

21/9 ▶ Who did Thabo Mbeki succeed as South African president in 1999?

21/10 ▶ 'Scrat' is an acorn-obsessed animal in what series of animated films?

21/11 ▶ Since June 1973 it's been compulsory for UK motor cyclists to wear what?

21/12 ▶ Which Welsh designer succeeded Alexander McQueen as chief designer at Givenchy?

21/13 ▶ Officially called 'The Monument of Light', The Spire is found in what EU capital?

21/14 ▶ Nancy and Bet are characters in what Lionel Bart musical?

21/15 ▶ 'As if by magic the shopkeeper appeared' was heard in what kids' TV programme?

Cash Builder Quiz 22

22/1 ▶ Adela Quested visits the subcontinent in what E M Forster novel?

22/2 ▶ In pantomime, at what type of event did Cinderella meet Prince Charming?

22/3 ▶ The Truman Balcony is on the second floor of what Washington residence?

22/4 ▶ Aleksandra Grabowska is the birth name of which *Strictly Come Dancing* performer?

22/5 ▶ What Asian city will host the 2020 Paralympics?

22/6 ▶ What term is used for the fee charged to use a bridge or section of road?

22/7 ▶ Joel Kinnaman is the title role policeman in a 2014 remake of what film?

22/8 ▶ The slogan 'The best to you each morning' originally advertised what company's breakfast cereal?

22/9 ▶ The Victims is the official fan club of what US rock band?

22/10 ▶ The name of what type of property comes from the French for 'small house'?

22/11 ▶ Granny Weatherwax is a character in what series of Terry Pratchett books?

22/12 ▶ Gibbons are the smallest members of what family of animals?

22/13 ▶ What Merseyside group split up in 1970 just before the release of *Let It Be*?

22/14 ▶ In 2012, South Africa released banknotes with which leader's image?

22/15 ▶ What type of venue are the Liverpool Empire and Birmingham Hippodrome?

Cash Builder Quiz 23

23/1 ▶ *My Autobiography* is the 2013 book by which ex-Manchester United boss?

23/2 ▶ The comedian James Anthony Patrick Carr is better known by what name?

23/3 ▶ During the First World War, which cabinet minister drowned on HMS *Hampshire* in 1916?

23/4 ▶ Traditionally, the Dutch shoes known as *klompen* are made from what?

23/5 ▶ Botticelli's fresco *Temptations of Christ* is on the wall of what chapel?

23/6 ▶ Which former champion was defeated on the first day of Wimbledon 2013?

23/7 ▷ What number follows 'East' and 'Heaven' to give the names of two chart bands?

23/8 ▷ Who was the US President at the start of the American Civil War?

23/9 ▷ If you're in a precarious situation you're said to be 'on thin...' what?

23/10 ▷ 'Bisque' is a seafood soup originally from what country's cuisine?

23/11 ▷ Which British dramatist wrote the plays *No Man's Land* and *Landscape*?

23/12 ▷ The Admiralty Board is an administrator of which of the armed services?

23/13 ▷ The most powerful person in what organisation calls himself *Capo di tutti capi*?

23/14 ▶ Who starred as a rapper called Alien in the 2012 film *Spring Breakers*?

23/15 ▶ Which Microsoft billionaire wrote the book *Business at the Speed of Thought*?

Cash Builder Quiz 24

24/1 ▶ What name for a German wine is also a joint on a horse's leg?

24/2 ▶ Mount Robson is the highest peak in the Canadian part of what mountain range?

24/3 ▶ 'Odd One Out' and 'Missing Words' are rounds on what current affairs panel show?

24/4 ▶ Kitty Packenham married which soldier and statesman in 1806?

24/5 ▶ What punctuation mark appears in the words 'don't' and 'won't'?

24/6 ▶ Yogi Bear's fictional home takes its name from what US National Park?

24/7 ▶ 'Other Side of Love' was a 2013 hit for which Grammy-winning singer?

24/8 ▶ Who is the only Swiss tennis player to have won the French Open men's singles?

24/9 ▶ From 1998 to 2005, Gerhard Schröder was Chancellor of what country?

24/10 ▶ Ralph Rackstraw and Josephine are characters in what Gilbert & Sullivan operetta?

24/11 ▶ What hospital department completes the name of the TV show *24 Hours in...*?

24/12 ▶ The Spanish hero called *El Campeador* is better known by what other name?

24/13 ▶ In finance, the letters PPP stand for 'Public-Private...' what?

24/14 ▶ Earth and what other planet in our solar system have names beginning with a vowel?

24/15 ▶ Anthony Head's character was a member of the Watchers' Council in what TV series?

Cash Builder Quiz 25

25/1 ▶ What word follows slumber, toga and tea to make the names of social gatherings?

25/2 ▶ Which antiques expert presents the afternoon show *Real Deal*?

25/3 ▶ What famous novel includes a chapter called 'D'Artagnan Shows Himself'?

25/4 ▶ Which island in the English Channel first held its annual music festival in 1968?

25/5 ▶ Highbury is the former home of what London football team?

25/6 ▶ Child actor Asa Butterfield played the title role in what 2011 Martin Scorsese film?

25/7 ▶ The alliance of two or more political parties to form a government is called what?

25/8 ▶ Tom Buchanan suspects his wife of an affair in what F Scott Fitzgerald novel?

25/9 ▶ What strong herb flavours the French sauce *pistou*?

25/10 ▶ Native to the North Pacific Ocean, what sort of creature is a surfperch?

25/11 ▶ What famous artefact was discovered by a French soldier in Egypt in 1799?

25/12 ▶ What widely used European currency is divided into one hundred cents?

25/13 ▶ Trinity College Cambridge won the 2014 final of what TV quiz show?

25/14 ▶ What Boyzone hit had already been a Number One for the Osmonds?

25/15 ▶ Slovakia and Switzerland both have capital cities beginning with what letter?

Cash Builder Quiz 26

26/1 ▶ What part of the oak tree is held in a cup-like structure called a cupule?

26/2 ▶ What American city is dubbed 'The Biggest Little City in the World'?

26/3 ▶ Played by Charlie Higson, office joker Colin Hunt was a character in what TV series?

26/4 ▶ What pizza delivery business is named after its founder John Schnatter?

26/5 ▶ At the start of a frame of snooker, what colour ball is positioned closest to the reds?

26/6 ▶ Bob Hoskins starred alongside cartoon characters in what '80s film?

26/7 ▶ A phrase for a large number of people is 'the world and his...' what?

26/8 ▶ Which Irish pop twins appeared on *Celebrity Big Brother* in 2011?

26/9 ▶ The disorder porphyria is thought to have caused the madness of which king?

26/10 ▶ In the name of the political party UKIP what does the IP stand for?

26/11 ▶ Which solo singer won his first Grammy for 'Don't Stop 'til You Get Enough'?

26/12 ▶ What imperial volume is roughly equal to 455 centilitres?

26/13 ▶ To which of her husbands was Elizabeth Taylor married the longest?

26/14 ▶ Crayola created a crayon called 'The Color Purple' for what talk-show host?

26/15 ▶ What Swiss chocolate comes in a lilac wrapper with a cow on it?

Cash Builder Quiz 27

27/1 ▶ *The Painter on His Way to Work* is a lost 1888 work by which Dutch painter?

27/2 ▶ Complete the name of the 1941 film starring Ginger Rogers: *Tom, Dick and...?*

27/3 ▶ 'Tawny' is a shade of what colour?

27/4 ▶ 'Stay The Night' was a 2014 hit for Zedd and featured which member of Paramore?

27/5 ▶ What party did Norman Tebbit represent in the House of Commons?

27/6 ▶ In 2012, the James Bond film franchise celebrated what anniversary?

27/7 ▶ Whose poem 'This be the Verse' has a very rude first line about parents?

27/8 ▶ Someone described as a 'tipster' is usually associated with what sport?

27/9 ▶ Claudius poisons the father of which Shakespeare title character?

CASH BUILDER QUESTIONS

27/10 ▶ What country is the setting for Disney's *Beauty and the Beast*?

27/11 ▶ What awards started as the 'British Record Industry Britannia Centenary Awards'?

27/12 ▶ What Northern Irish distillery makes the whiskey Black Bush?

27/13 ▶ What would you be most likely to see in a hanging basket?

27/14 ▶ Famously worn by punks, what fastening device was invented by Walter Hunt?

27/15 ▶ Coach on TV show *The Voice UK*, Ricky Wilson is the lead singer of what band?

Cash Builder Quiz 28

28/1 ▶ The short story 'Snow, Glass, Apples' is based on what fairy tale?

28/2 ▶ In astronomy, the Carina, Eagle and Cone are what type of gas and dust cloud?

28/3 ▶ Who is the only rower to have been BBC Sports Personality of the Year?

28/4 ▶ 'Cracklin' Rosie' was the first British hit for which American singer?

28/5 ▶ Who led the 26th of July revolutionary movement in Cuba?

28/6 ▶ Thomas More, Guy Fawkes and Rudolf Hess were all imprisoned in what fortress?

28/7 ▶ In a Frank Sinatra song, it's 'one for my baby, and one more for the...' what?

28/8 ▶ 'Fisherman's rib' is a knitting pattern used for making what items of clothing?

CASH BUILDER QUESTIONS

28/9 ▶ What surname links authors Jackie and Wilkie?

28/10 ▶ The lute belongs to what family of instruments?

28/11 ▶ What Ricky Gervais comedy centres on and stars actor Warwick Davis?

28/12 ▶ What 'M' is the name of a UK airline and a species of butterfly?

28/13 ▶ Aunt Em is the last character named in what L Frank Baum novel?

28/14 ▶ What was the first name of the physicist after whom Hooke's Law is named?

28/15 ▶ In the West End début of the musical *Matilda*, which female character was played by a man?

Cash Builder Quiz 29

29/1 ▶ Alpha and what other Greek letter feature in the phonetic alphabet?

29/2 ▶ Complete the advertising slogan 'Beanz Meanz...' what?

29/3 ▶ The song 'Shake' was the only solo chart single for which former Wham! member?

29/4 ▶ What nickname for Margaret Thatcher was inspired by a King of the Huns?

29/5 ▶ The capital cities of Poland and the US both begin with what letter?

29/6 ▶ From 1914 the Ford Model T motor car was mass-produced in what colour?

29/7 ▶ In 1982, which American businesswoman published her first book *Entertaining*?

CASH BUILDER QUESTIONS

29/8 ▶ What country of the UK had three kings called Constantine?

29/9 ▶ What Nintendo video-game character wears a green cap with the letter 'L' on it?

29/10 ▶ In what film does Jodie Foster hide with her daughter in a vault-like part of her home?

29/11 ▶ Caldas and Risaralda in Colombia are areas for growing beans of what beverage?

29/12 ▶ The Suez Crisis followed the American and British decision not to finance what dam?

29/13 ▶ Football pundits Alan Hansen and Mark Lawrenson both played for what team?

29/14 ▶ Mister Dose the Doctor and his wife and children feature in what card game?

29/15 ▶ *Tattoos* is a 2013 album by which American singer?

Cash Builder Quiz 30

30/1 ▶ On regular six-sided dice, what number is on the opposite side to six?

30/2 ▶ *Hurricane Gold* is the fourth book to feature a young version of what spy?

30/3 ▶ What traditional Asian board game is played on a grid of 19 by 19?

30/4 ▶ What South American country shares its name with a Terry Gilliam film?

30/5 ▶ Florence is the capital of what Italian region?

30/6 ▶ Mr Wickham is a character in what Jane Austen novel?

30/7 ▶ Which Wimbledon champion appeared in the 75th anniversary issue of the *Beano*?

30/8 ▶ Found on old Chinese porcelain, *sang-de-bœuf* is a shade of what primary colour?

30/9 ▶ The David Attenborough TV series *Life in the Freezer* is about what continent?

30/10 ▶ Eggs and what other dairy product are vital ingredients of Yorkshire pudding?

30/11 ▶ *I'd Do Anything* was a talent show to find leads in what musical?

30/12 ▶ What J D Salinger book opens with the words 'If you really want to hear about it...'?

30/13 ▶ Glueball, Donk and Tyrus set what puzzles in *The Independent* newspaper?

30/14 ▶ The first crossing of the Atlantic by hot-air balloon was in what century?

30/15 ▶ Which American pop star co-stars in the 2013 film *Thanks for Sharing*?

Cash Builder Quiz 31

31/1 ▶ John, Bobby and Ted were members of what American political dynasty?

31/2 ▶ What Beijing palace acquired its name as most people were not allowed into it?

31/3 ▶ In 1963, Valentina Tereshkova became the first woman to go where?

31/4 ▶ Jock and Yorkie are friends of what comic strip dog?

31/5 ▶ What global chain of chicken restaurants was founded in South Africa in 1987?

CASH BUILDER QUESTIONS

31/6 ▶ What London airport is based in an Essex resort?

31/7 ▶ *The Hungarian Rhapsodies* are a group of 19 piano pieces by which composer?

31/8 ▶ What Apollo mission was the subject of a 1995 film?

31/9 ▶ Which TV baker released the cookbook *Family Sunday Lunches*?

31/10 ▶ The process of 'hydraulic fracturing' is also known by what one-word name?

31/11 ▶ Classical mythology is usually seen as the myths of the Greeks and which people?

31/12 ▶ Which film in the *Fast and Furious* series was released in 2013?

31/13 ▶ The flag of Saudi Arabia features a quote from what religious work?

31/14 ▶ Offa's Dyke traditionally separates England from what other country of the UK?

31/15 ▶ What French company produces the Elvive line of hair-care products?

Cash Builder Quiz 32

32/1 ▶ The Taylor Swift hit 'Everything Has Changed' features which British singer?

32/2 ▶ What's the only species of big cat that lives in a large group rather than in solitude?

32/3 ▶ What's the name of Uncle Henry's niece in *The Wizard of Oz*?

32/4 ▶ Nurse Jennifer Worth's memoirs are the basis of what TV drama series?

CASH BUILDER QUESTIONS

32/5 ▶ What 12-month break is taken by some students between school and university?

32/6 ▶ Which King of Macedonia deposed the Persian ruler Darius the Third?

32/7 ▶ Jason Leonard won over a hundred caps for England in what sport?

32/8 ▶ What word means both a chest and the main part of a tree?

32/9 ▶ Beyoncé covered Amy Winehouse's *Back to Black* for the soundtrack to what film?

32/10 ▶ In an athletics result, what does PB beside a name mean?

32/11 ▶ Which cartoon sailor was Elzie Segar's most famous creation?

32/12 ▶ The founder of what French fashion brand was nicknamed 'The Crocodile'?

32/13 ▶ A tendency to infidelity is said to happen after how many years of marriage?

32/14 ▶ Who starred as Julianne Potter in the film *My Best Friend's Wedding*?

32/15 ▶ What 600-ft tall tower opened at the World's Fair in Seattle in 1962?

Cash Builder Quiz 33

33/1 ▶ Corona beer is from what North American country?

33/2 ▶ What's three-fifths of 20?

33/3 ▶ What search engine company owns the photo-sharing service Flickr?

CASH BUILDER QUESTIONS

33/4 ▶ Which former *X Factor* contestant supported Robbie Williams on his 2013 tour?

33/5 ▶ Frenchman Camille Pissarro was a key figure in what art movement?

33/6 ▶ At weddings, what staple food is sometimes thrown instead of confetti?

33/7 ▶ Balls used in what sport are lying on the Moon?

33/8 ▶ Who had a Number One hit in 2013 with her debut single 'Royals'?

33/9 ▶ Basalt rocks form what World Heritage Site in Northern Ireland?

33/10 ▶ Violet and Veruca are characters in what Roald Dahl novel?

33/11 ▶ What relation was King Edward the Seventh to Kaiser Wilhelm the Second?

33/12 ▶ Who starred as Captain Billy Tyne in the film *The Perfect Storm*?

33/13 ▶ The Gulf States are countries that border what arm of the Arabian Sea?

33/14 ▶ What season of the year ends at the vernal equinox?

33/15 ▶ The Purple One and Orange Crunch feature in what chocolate selection box?

Cash Builder Quiz 34

34/1 ▶ Which son of the Queen served on HMS *Invincible* in the Falklands War?

34/2 ▶ On what gameshow did Dale Winton tell contestants to go 'wild in the aisles'?

34/3 ▶ What Scottish town is named after a well dedicated to the Virgin Mary?

34/4 ▶ *Fairy Tales Told for Children* were 19th-century books by which Dane?

34/5 ▶ 'Thronies' are fans of what fantasy TV drama?

34/6 ▶ What word can be a bump on a ski slope or an important person in the film industry?

34/7 ▶ What became the national currency of Estonia in 2011?

34/8 ▶ Which future US President was in charge of Allied forces on D-day?

34/9 ▶ In the famous Vermeer painting what is the girl's earring made of?

QUIZ 33–34

34/10 ▶ In *EastEnders*, how was Margaret Ann Mitchell better known?

34/11 ▶ In Indian cuisine, a pakora is cooked by what method?

34/12 ▶ On what night is Ant and Dec's *TV Takeaway*?

34/13 ▶ In the 'Desperate Dan' comic strip, what pie has horns coming out of the pastry?

34/14 ▶ In total, 623 people appear on what 11th-century embroidery?

34/15 ▶ What mischievous sprite get its name from the Old Irish for 'small body'?

Cash Builder Quiz 35

35/1 ▶ In what racket sport is a 'stop volley' played close to the net?

CASH BUILDER QUESTIONS

35/2 ▶ In the mid-1980s, who played Jenna Wade in the soap *Dallas*?

35/3 ▶ Grenache Noir is a grape used to make what colour wine?

35/4 ▶ An EEG measures electrical activity in what part of the body?

35/5 ▶ On what road in Chelsea did Mary Quant open her boutique 'Bazaar'?

35/6 ▶ What Ultravox song was voted the UK's favourite Number Two single in 2012?

35/7 ▶ What first name links the novelists Faulkner and Golding?

35/8 ▶ In accepting both good and bad times, you are said to 'take the rough with...' what?

35/9 ▶ Actors with the surnames 'Reeve' and 'Reeves' have played which superhero on screen?

35/10 ▶ Who is the only snooker player to have won BBC Sports Personality of the Year?

35/11 ▶ What board game introduced a baseball bat as a possible weapon in 2008?

35/12 ▶ What airline ran the Concorde advert 'Breakfast in London. Lunch in New York'?

35/13 ▶ Rapper Lisa Maffia was once a member of what South London hip-hop group?

35/14 ▶ Thomas More opposed Henry the Eighth's divorce from which queen?

35/15 ▶ According to Spanish law, what fortified wine can only be produced in Jerez?

Cash Builder Quiz 36

36/1 ▶ 'Spaceship Earth' is a giant geosphere at what Florida theme park?

36/2 ▶ A 'Cupid's bow' may be found on what part of the face?

36/3 ▶ A mechanical rodeo bull ride is also called a 'bucking...' what?

36/4 ▶ What word was the title of 2013 hits for both The Saturdays and Psy?

36/5 ▶ Four-dimensional space-time is a central concept in what Einstein theory?

36/6 ▶ What cartoon family are described as 'a page right out of history'?

36/7 ▶ Samoa gained independence from what Commonwealth country in 1962?

36/8 ▶ In an Italian restaurant at what course would you usually eat *gelato*?

36/9 ▶ In 1982, who was flat racing Champion Jockey for the 11th and last time?

36/10 ▶ Which actress played the Black Widow in the 2012 film *Avengers Assemble*?

36/11 ▶ In English tradition there will be 40 days of rain if it rains on what saint's day?

36/12 ▶ If you are running out of patience, you are said to be 'at the end of your...' what?

36/13 ▶ What sign of the zodiac is linked to the crab that pinched Heracles in Greek myth?

36/14 ▶ Who directed the 1939 film version of Daphne Du Maurier's *Jamaica Inn*?

36/15 ▶ The title of which 1980 Kate Bush hit means 'grandmother' in Russian?

Cash Builder Quiz 37

37/1 ▶ Cast in 1881, the largest single bell in the UK is in what London cathedral?

37/2 ▶ Words having the same sound but different meanings are called what?

37/3 ▶ *Managing My Life* is the autobiography of what football manager?

37/4 ▶ Emilia Clarke plays the 'Mother of Dragons' in what fantasy TV series?

37/5 ▶ Who collaborated with Friedrich Engels on *The Communist Manifesto*?

37/6 ▶ Added to *Oxford Dictionaries* online in 2012, 'ridic' is short for what word?

37/7 ▶ The Bedser Stand is at what England Test cricket ground?

37/8 ▶ What cap with a large peak is named after a North American sport?

37/9 ▶ The names of the two largest Dutch cities both end in what three letters?

37/10 ▶ What is the occupation of Peter Parker, the alter ego of Spider-Man?

37/11 ▶ First used to make stockings in 1940, what was the first fully synthetic polymer textile?

37/12 ▶ What place for cleaning vehicles is the title of a disco song by Rose Royce?

37/13 ▶ The Ural river flows through Kazakhstan and what other country?

37/14 ▶ In 2006, NASA launched the New Horizons spacecraft intended to reach what dwarf planet?

37/15 ▶ 'It's Alright' is the theme song of what TV crime drama?

Cash Builder Quiz 38

38/1 ▶ Which Scottish actor stars in the action film *Olympus Has Fallen*?

38/2 ▶ Which snooker player won his fifth Masters title in 2014?

38/3 ▶ The 'soul arch' is a classic manoeuvre in what water activity?

38/4 ▶ What word is used to describe an object that does not let any light pass through it?

38/5 ▶ Pop star Ricky Martin has released albums in English and what other language?

38/6 ▶ In the 1970s, the US engaged in so-called 'ping pong diplomacy' with what country?

38/7 ▶ The full name of the C S Lewis book is *Prince Caspian: The Return to...* where?

38/8 ▶ What word for an extreme scarcity of food comes from the Latin for hunger?

38/9 ▶ Jason Statham plays a former DEA agent in what 2013 film?

38/10 ▶ In 2005, Reuters was the last major news group to leave what London street?

38/11 ▶ Which physicist is credited with saying 'coincidence is God's way of remaining anonymous'?

38/12 ▶ Which celebrity chef opened the Union Jacks restaurant in Covent Garden?

38/13 ▶ A 'couchette' is a carriage with sleeping berths used on what form of transport?

38/14 ▶ You won't get into trouble, if you keep on the 'straight and...' what?

38/15 ▶ Robin Cook called what Indian food 'a true British national dish'?

Cash Builder Quiz 39

39/1 ▶ A car with the number plate 'A.U.One' appears in what James Bond film?

39/2 ▶ Referring to being given the push, what does the 'E' stand for in 'The Big E'?

39/3 ▶ What citrus fruit became the state fruit of Florida in 2005?

39/4 ▶ What fictional river appears in the title of a George Eliot novel?

39/5 ▷ How many General Elections did Neil Kinnock lose as Labour Party leader?

39/6 ▷ 'Gorgeous Gussie' was the nickname of which tennis player of the 1940s?

39/7 ▷ Baroness Schraeder and Uncle Max are characters in what musical?

39/8 ▷ The mouth of the River Tweed is in what country of the UK?

39/9 ▷ What Mexican snack is an anagram of the word 'coat'?

39/10 ▷ Al Capone was released from what famous American prison in 1939?

39/11 ▷ What blood-sucking creature was the *Looney Tunes* character Count Bloodcount?

39/12 ▶ What type of storm do Americans refer to as a 'twister'?

39/13 ▶ Who presents the TV show *The Big Allotment Challenge*?

39/14 ▶ What word for a criminal can also mean 'poorly' in Australian English?

39/15 ▶ In the rhyme 'Ride a Cock Horse', the lady is on a horse of what colour?

Cash Builder Quiz 40

40/1 ▶ What Apollo mission was the final rehearsal for the first Moon landing?

40/2 ▶ What Gloria Gaynor hit is the only song to win a Grammy for Best Disco Recording?

40/3 ▶ Ultraviolet radiation produces what vitamin in the skin?

QUIZ 39–40

40/4 ▷ In the film *Shrek 2*, whose nose grows when he denies wearing ladies underwear?

40/5 ▷ A process carried out to satisfy rules is said to be an exercise of ticking what?

40/6 ▷ Petits fours are cakes usually served after dinner with what hot drink?

40/7 ▷ Which coach from *The Voice UK* provides the voice of Pedro in the film *Rio Two*?

40/8 ▷ What Spanish football team has been European champion 10 times?

40/9 ▷ What rebuilt London church opened for services in 1697?

40/10 ▷ In the Nintendo video game series, what is the name of Luigi's brother?

CASH BUILDER QUESTIONS

40/11 ▶ What Neil Simon musical is subtitled *The Adventures of a Girl Who Wanted to Be Loved*?

40/12 ▶ What zodiac sign is represented by a maiden carrying a sheaf of wheat?

40/13 ▶ What Ricky Gervais TV series is set at the Broadhill retirement home?

40/14 ▶ Who was British Prime Minister for just 12 months in the 1960s?

40/15 ▶ In a fairy tale, whose name comes from a French word for 'Little Cinders'?

HEAD TO HEAD

HEAD

QUESTIONS

Q

HEAD TO HEAD WITH

The

GOVERNESS

Head to Head – The Governess Quiz 1

1/1 ▶ Olympic swimmer Ian Thorpe is allergic to what chemical element?

> **A** Mercury **B** Iron **C** Chlorine

1/2 ▶ Which of these words does NOT feature in the title of a hit song by Shakira?

> **A** Whatever **B** Whenever **C** Wherever

1/3 ▶ Crucifixes and holy water are meant to repel what legendary creatures?

> **A** Fairies **B** Vampires **C** Witches

1/4 ▶ What name is shared by characters in the musicals *Hairspray* and *Chicago*?

> **A** Roxie **B** Tracy **C** Velma

1/5 ▶ Which of these moons of Neptune orbits the planet in the opposite direction to the others?

> **A** Triton **B** Larissa **C** Nereid

1/6 ▶ Which of these imaginary lines lies largely at 180 degrees longitude?

> **A** Equator **B** International Date Line **C** Tropic of Cancer

1/7 ▶ The two major Tibetan Buddhist sects are called the red and yellow... what?

> **A** Belts   **B** Hats   **C** Robes

1/8 ▶ The Cornish cheese Yarg is coated with the leaves of what plant?

> **A** Chestnut   **B** Fig   **C** Nettle

1/9 ▶ Additional demands that a touring musician ensures are added to a basic contract are known as what?

> **A** Riders   **B** Drivers   **C** Jockeys

1/10 ▶ Who did Virginia Wade beat to win the Wimbledon Ladies' Singles title?

> **A** Betty Stove   **B** Martina Navratilova   **C** Billie Jean King

1/11 ▶ How many symphonies did Johannes Brahms write?

> **A** Two   **B** Four   **C** Eight

1/12 ▶ The manoeuvre in which a car is rapidly turned in a complete circle is known as what?

> **A** Bagel   **B** Doughnut   **C** Eclair

QUIZ 1

Head to Head – The Governess Quiz 2

2/1 ▶ Pomegranate is traditionally used to make which of these?

> **A** Angostura bitters **B** Sour mix **C** Grenadine

2/2 ▶ Elizabeth I turned down the crown of which of these countries?

> **A** Netherlands **B** Portugal **C** Sweden

2/3 ▶ What mathematical term comes from the Latin word for 'broken'?

> **A** Division **B** Fraction **C** Subtraction

2/4 ▶ The 2013 America's Cup took place off the coast of which California city?

> **A** San Diego **B** Santa Monica **C** San Francisco

2/5 ▶ During the digestion process, the stomach turns food into a semifluid mixture called what?

> **A** Chyme **B** Spume **C** Brome

2/6 ▶ What does the word 'Olympus' refer to in the title of the film *Olympus Has Fallen*?

> **A** The White House **B** Fort Knox **C** The Pentagon

2/7 ▶ 'No matter how hard I try' is the opening line of what Cher song?

> **A** 'Believe'   **B** 'If I Could Turn Back Time'   **C** 'Just Like Jesse James'

2/8 ▶ Firefox is an alternative name for what animal?

> **A** Flying squirrel   **B** Red panda   **C** Bush baby

2/9 ▶ The Speaker of the House of Commons is selected by whom?

> **A** The Queen   **B** The Prime Minister   **C** MPs

2/10 ▶ In the Ottawan song 'D.I.S.C.O.', which of these words is used to describe the girl in the lyrics?

> **A** Delicious   **B** Sensational   **C** Constipated

2/11 ▶ A speciality of Normandy cuisine, what French delicacies are *andouillettes*?

> **A** Boiled chicken feet   **B** Fried bull testicles   **C** Pig intestine sausages

2/12 ▶ Which of these National Parks does NOT have a coastline?

> **A** Exmoor   **B** Lake District   **C** Yorkshire Dales

QUIZ 2

Head to Head – The Governess Quiz 3

3/1 ▷ In the novels by Bernard Cornwell, what is Sharpe's first name?

> **A** Raymond **B** Richard **C** Robert

3/2 ▷ Mae West claimed 'Love conquers all things except poverty and...' what?

> **A** Infidelity **B** Hunger **C** Toothache

3/3 ▷ Sir Miles Axlerod and Holly Shiftwell are characters in which Pixar film?

> **A** *Cars 2* **B** *Monsters University* **C** *Toy Story 2*

3/4 ▷ Which of these cartoon strips does NOT appear in the *Daily Mirror*?

> **A** The Perishers **B** Andy Capp **C** Fred Basset

3/5 ▷ Which of these is a first language for the largest number of people?

> **A** French **B** German **C** Italian

3/6 ▷ Which of these craftsmen would be most likely to make use of a 'tenon and mortise'?

> **A** Printer **B** Cobbler **C** Carpenter

3/7 ▷ In the 1951 Ronald Reagan film *Bedtime for Bonzo*, what is Bonzo?

> **A** Leopard **B** Donkey **C** Chimpanzee

3/8 ▷ What was the only UK Number One single from Michael Jackson's *Thriller* album?

> **A** 'Billie Jean' **B** 'Beat It' **C** 'The Girl is Mine'

3/9 ▷ In the game of Bridge, what is a hand with no trumps?

> **A** Straight **B** Bend **C** Chicane

3/10 ▷ The vertical side of a doorway or window is called a what?

> **A** Gable **B** Jamb **C** Tread

3/11 ▷ What relation are Peepeye, Poopeye and Pupeye to Popeye?

> **A** Sons **B** Brothers **C** Nephews

3/12 ▷ The stately home of Blenheim Palace is in a small town called what?

> **A** Glyndebourne **B** Sherborne **C** Woodstock

QUIZ 3

Head to Head – The Governess Quiz 4

4/1 ▶ Which of these countries has the most time zones?

> **A** China **B** India **C** Russia

4/2 ▶ Which famously forgetful writer once sent a telegram to his wife 'Am in Market Harborough. Where ought I to be?'?

> **A** G K Chesterton **B** T S Eliot **C** D H Lawrence

4/3 ▶ Dubbin is used to soften and waterproof what?

> **A** Leather **B** Wool **C** Silk

4/4 ▶ In the human body, the 'hallux' is better known as what?

> **A** Little finger **B** Big toe **C** Thumb

4/5 ▶ Which of these countries has a square flag?

> **A** Faroe Islands **B** Luxembourg **C** Vatican City

4/6 ▶ In the TV show *Batman,* who was the only other person to know the true identities of the Dynamic Duo?

> **A** Alfred **B** Commissioner Gordon **C** Aunt Harriet

4/7 ▶ Which athlete set three world records and equalled a fourth on the same day in 1935?

> **A** Jesse Owens **B** Babe Didrikson **C** Fanny Blankers-Koen

4/8 ▷ Which of these is the name of a river in Cumbria?

> **A** Cornwall **B** Essex **C** Kent

4/9 ▷ The misprinted *Wicked Bible* of 1631 declares 'Thou shall commit...' what?

> **A** Adultery **B** Blasphemy **C** Murder

4/10 ▷ Which former member of JLS became a co-presenter on *The Voice UK* in 2014?

> **A** Aston **B** JB **C** Marvin

4/11 ▷ Noël Coward's comedy *Blithe Spirit* takes its title from a line by which poet?

> **A** Keats **B** Shelley **C** Wordsworth

4/12 ▷ What name is given to a first-year student at an American high school or university?

> **A** Freshman **B** Junior **C** Sophomore

QUIZ 4

Head to Head – The Governess Quiz 5

5/1 ▶ Which country abolished its monarchy in 2008?

> **A** Nepal **B** Nicaragua **C** North Korea

5/2 ▶ What gold coin of 240 grains was first issued under Henry VII?

> **A** Groat **B** Sovereign **C** Ducat

5/3 ▶ Born on St Valentine's Day 2014, what name did Simon Cowell and Lauren Silverman give to their new baby?

> **A** Cyril **B** Walter **C** Eric

5/4 ▶ According to the title of a 2014 novel, what did the 'Little Old Lady' do?

> **A** Broke All the Rules **B** Climbed Out of the Window **C** Ate All the Cheese

5/5 ▶ Which of these is the name of a mountain in Greece?

> **A** Mount Athos **B** Mount Porthos **C** Mount Aramis

5/6 ▶ What is the highest singing voice in women and boys?

> **A** Contralto **B** Alto **C** Soprano

5/7 ▶ The 2009 film *The Young Victoria* was based on an idea by whom?

> **A** Sarah Ferguson **B** Princess Anne **C** The Queen

5/8 ▶ Which of these countries was NOT among the Allied powers during the First World War?

> **A** Japan **B** Italy **C** Turkey

5/9 ▶ A ruby wedding anniversary celebrates how many years of marriage?

> **A** 25 **B** 40 **C** 50

5/10 ▶ Which of these actresses was first to win an Oscar?

> **A** Maggie Smith **B** Meryl Streep **C** Mary Steenburgen

5/11 ▶ What Shakespeare character says the line 'False face must hide what the false heart doth know'?

> **A** Romeo **B** Iago **C** Macbeth

5/12 ▶ Boulder City in Nevada was developed to house the workers creating what project?

> **A** Hoover Dam **B** Las Vegas Airport **C** Mount Rushmore

QUIZ 5

Head to Head – The Governess Quiz 6

6/1 ▶ In folklore, which of these is the name of a member of Robin Hood's band of men?

A Basil of Barnsley **B** David of Doncaster **C** Rodney of Rotherham

6/2 ▶ American soldiers in the First World War were given what nickname?

A Bagelheads **B** Doughboys **C** Burgerbums

6/3 ▶ Which of these world capitals is on the coast?

A Brasilia **B** Bridgetown **C** Brussels

6/4 ▶ What name is given to a cocktail made with lemon juice, sugar and a spirit such as brandy or gin?

A Shoot **B** Pitch **C** Sling

6/5 ▶ In 2014, which group became the first act to sell six million copies of an individual album in the UK?

A Dire Straits **B** One Direction **C** Queen

6/6 ▶ Which author served as a Democrat in the Mississippi House of Representatives from 1984 until 1990?

A John Grisham **B** Stephen King **C** Tom Clancy

6/7 ▶ The Latin phrase *modus operandi* means what?

A Time flies   B Voice of the people   C Way of operating

6/8 ▶ What can be measured in both degrees and radians?

A Angles   B Temperature   C Volume

6/9 ▶ What name has been used by three Scottish Kings, seven Popes, one Antipope and three Russian Tsars?

A Malcolm   B Alexander   C Nicholas

6/10 ▶ Which scientist featured on the £1 note between 1978 and 1988?

A Humphry Davy   B Alexander Graham Bell   C Isaac Newton

6/11 ▶ Which singer had Number One albums with 'From Now On' and 'Friday's Child'?

A Leona Lewis   B Shayne Ward   C Will Young

6/12 ▶ The Long Island Sound separates New York from what other state?

A Connecticut   B Delaware   C Maryland

Head to Head – The Governess Quiz 7

7/1 ▶ An emblem of a leek is most likely to be worn on the feast day of which patron saint?

> **A** Saint David   **B** Saint Patrick   **C** Saint Andrew

7/2 ▶ The writer Simone de Beauvoir was the long-time companion of which Frenchman?

> **A** Charles de Gaulle   **B** Eric Cantona   **C** Jean-Paul Sartre

7/3 ▶ In what event did Kelly Gallagher win Britain's first ever Winter Paralympic gold medal?

> **A** Super G   **B** Women's downhill   **C** Grand slalom

7/4 ▶ Who stepped down as leader of the Liberal Democrats in 1999?

> **A** Paddy Ashdown   **B** David Steel   **C** Charles Kennedy

7/5 ▶ Where does a priest wear a *zucchetto*?

> **A** On his feet   **B** Around his waist   **C** On his head

7/6 ▶ Which of these features in the title of a bestselling Deborah Rodriguez novel?

> **A** Sweet Shop   **B** Coffee Shop   **C** Joke Shop

HEAD-TO-HEAD QUESTIONS – THE GOVERNESS

7/7 ▶ Which footballer said 'If I had been born ugly, you would have never heard of Pelé'?

> **A** Diego Maradona   **B** George Best   **C** Johan Cruyff

7/8 ▶ Which of these wars took place first?

> **A** Six Day War   **B** Seven Weeks' War   **C** Thirty Years' War

7/9 ▶ Where in Australia is Uluru or Ayers Rock?

> **A** Northern Territory   **B** Western Australia   **C** South Australia

7/10 ▶ Enid Blyton's Famous Five had how many legs in total?

> **A** 10   **B** 12   **C** 14

7/11 ▶ Which of these was NOT Chancellor of the Exchequer during Margaret Thatcher's premiership?

> **A** Nigel Lawson   **B** John Major   **C** Norman Lamont

7/12 ▶ Which of these islands is the largest?

> **A** Jersey   **B** Isle of Man   **C** Skye

Head to Head – The Governess Quiz 8

8/1 ▷ Where would you be most likely to see the phenomenon called St Elmo's Fire?

> **A** At sea **B** In space **C** Underground

8/2 ▷ Which of these courses does NOT hold one of the five horse-racing classics?

> **A** Epsom **B** Newmarket **C** Ascot

8/3 ▷ The astrological year begins on the 21st of what month?

> **A** March **B** June **C** December

8/4 ▷ Which of these national flags does NOT feature red and white stripes?

> **A** Kazakhstan **B** Liberia **C** Malaysia

8/5 ▷ According to the proverb, 'An Englishman's home is his...' what?

> **A** Castle **B** Kingdom **C** Millstone

8/6 ▷ The Pacific Ocean contains approximately what percentage of the world's water?

> **A** 36% **B** 46% **C** 56%

8/7 ▶ Which author broke her engagement with Harris Bigg-Wither the day after she accepted his marriage proposal?

> **A** Jane Austen   **B** Charlotte Brontë   **C** George Eliot

8/8 ▶ Cousin Itt is a hairy relative of which fictional family?

> **A** The Partridge Family   **B** The Addams Family   **C** The Royle Family

8/9 ▶ In what county are Watford Gap motorway services?

> **A** Hertfordshire   **B** Lincolnshire   **C** Northamptonshire

8/10 ▶ The Greek architect Sostratus built which Wonder of the Ancient World?

> **A** Colossus of Rhodes   **B** Pharos of Alexandria   **C** Temple of Artemis

8/11 ▶ The dried variety of what fruit is traditionally used in a hot cross bun?

> **A** Apricot   **B** Grapes   **C** Plums

8/12 ▶ *The Holiday Home* is a novel by which TV presenter?

> **A** Fern Britton   **B** Tess Daly   **C** Gloria Hunniford

QUIZ 8

Head to Head – The Governess Quiz 9

9/1 ▶ What is the standard unit of atomic mass?

> **A** Dalton   **B** Galton   **C** Walton

9/2 ▶ In mythology, what objects are associated with the deity Eros?

> **A** Bow and arrow   **B** Ball and chain   **C** Bucket and spade

9/3 ▶ What desert did David Livingstone cross in 1849?

> **A** Atacama   **B** Gobi   **C** Kalahari

9/4 ▶ Which of these shipping forecast areas does NOT touch the British mainland?

> **A** Fair Isle   **B** Forth   **C** Forties

9/5 ▶ The background of Ferrari's black horse logo is what colour?

> **A** Yellow   **B** Green   **C** Blue

9/6 ▶ The Banksy work *Pulp Fiction Bananas* featured John Travolta and which actor?

> **A** Bruce Willis   **B** Steve Buscemi   **C** Samuel L Jackson

9/7 ▷ How wide is a hockey goal?

> **A** 8 feet **B** 10 feet **C** 12 feet

9/8 ▷ The International Criminal Court is based in which Dutch city?

> **A** Eindhoven **B** The Hague **C** Rotterdam

9/9 ▷ Which is the northernmost of these Channel Islands?

> **A** Alderney **B** Jersey **C** Sark

9/10 ▷ In geometry, the highest point of a solid figure relative to its base is called what?

> **A** Apex **B** Acme **C** Apogee

9/11 ▷ What part of a Basset hound is noticeably very long?

> **A** Legs **B** Snout **C** Ears

9/12 ▷ Which of these is a member of the band Rudimental?

> **A** DJ Locksmith **B** DJ Plumber **C** DJ Bricklayer

QUIZ 9

Head to Head – The Governess Quiz 10

10/1 ▶ The so-called 'acid test' comes from the testing of gold for purity using what?

> **A** Citric acid **B** Sulphuric acid **C** Nitric acid

10/2 ▶ The adjective 'Jovian' refers to which Roman god?

> **A** Jupiter **B** Mars **C** Mercury

10/3 ▶ What was the population of the US when George Washington was President?

> **A** 4 million **B** 24 million **C** 44 million

10/4 ▶ 'He had decided to live forever or die in the attempt' is a well-known quote from which novel?

> **A** *Brave New World* **B** *Catch-22* **C** *Nineteen Eighty-Four*

10/5 ▶ Which of these is the equivalent of three-quarters?

> **A** 6/12 **B** 8/12 **C** 9/12

10/6 ▶ Google Play distributes apps designed for what operating system?

> **A** iOS **B** Android **C** Windows

10/7 ▶ Which of these languages does NOT use a Cyrillic alphabet?

> **A** Macedonian   **B** Bulgarian   **C** Albanian

10/8 ▶ Which of these creatures is arboreal?

> **A** Hedgehog   **B** Koala   **C** Badger

10/9 ▶ What forest stretches through Brazil, Paraguay and Argentina?

> **A** Atlantic forest   **B** Pacific forest   **C** Antarctic forest

10/10 ▶ What gives tomatoes their red colour?

> **A** Lycopene   **B** Carotene   **C** Pectin

10/11 ▶ Which actor, who has played James Bond on screen, was once a lifeguard and a coffin polisher?

> **A** Pierce Brosnan   **B** Daniel Craig   **C** Sean Connery

10/12 ▶ Which of these boys' names does NOT end the name of a country?

> **A** Mark   **B** Stan   **C** Tony

HEAD TO HEAD WITH

The BEAST

Head to Head – The Beast Quiz 1

1/1 ▶ The Olympic swimmer known as 'Eric the Eel' came from what country?

> **A** Ecuador   **B** Equatorial Guinea   **C** Estonia

1/2 ▶ Who was the first woman to be paid $5 million for a film appearance?

> **A** Elizabeth Taylor   **B** Bette Midler   **C** Barbra Streisand

1/3 ▶ Which of these is a chocolate treat made with marshmallows?

> **A** Uneven Path   **B** Rocky Road   **C** Bumpy Lane

1/4 ▶ Which of the following literary characters did NOT converse with an animal?

> **A** Pippi Longstocking   **B** Mary Poppins   **C** Harry Potter

1/5 ▶ Which space shuttle flew the most missions?

> **A** Atlantis   **B** Discovery   **C** Endeavour

1/6 ▶ The bending of a light beam when it passes from one transparent medium to another is known as what?

> **A** Reflection   **B** Refraction   **C** Reflation

1/7 ▷ Crown Prince is an alternative name for which of these titles?

> **A** Heir Apparent   **B** Heir Presumptive   **C** Heir Assumed

1/8 ▷ Which of these musicals appeared on Broadway first?

> **A** *Avenue Q*   **B** *42nd Street*   **C** *Sunset Boulevard*

1/9 ▷ The cartoon character Dudley Do-right was a member of which police force?

> **A** The Mounties   **B** The NYPD   **C** The Met

1/10 ▷ In cocktail making, pressing a fruit or herb to release its flavour is called what?

> **A** Cuddling   **B** Fuddling   **C** Muddling

1/11 ▷ On a standard piano with 88 keys, how many are black?

> **A** 24   **B** 30   **C** 36

1/12 ▷ Mick Ronson was the guitarist with what band?

> **A** The Beetles from Venus   **B** The Spiders from Mars
> **C** The Crabs from Uranus

QUIZ 1

Head to Head – The Beast Quiz 2

2/1 ▶ What structures appear on the reverse of Euro banknotes?

> **A** Churches   **B** Bridges   **C** Castles

2/2 ▶ The rock formation known as the 'Devil's Marbles' is located in what country?

> **A** Brazil   **B** Australia   **C** Egypt

2/3 ▶ What force causes oceans to have tides?

> **A** Friction   **B** Gravity   **C** Momentum

2/4 ▶ Which former captain of the England rugby union team was nicknamed 'Bumface'?

> **A** Lewis Moody   **B** Martin Johnson   **C** Will Carling

2/5 ▶ Complete the title of Hergé's first ever Tintin adventure: *Tintin in the Land of the…*?

> **A** Americans   **B** Pharaohs   **C** Soviets

2/6 ▶ A member of which profession does NOT use the title 'Sir' if he is knighted?

> **A** Army   **B** Banking   **C** Clergy

2/7 ▶ Which of these performers was first to win an Oscar for playing a monarch?

> **A** Colin Firth   **B** Helen Mirren   **C** Judi Dench

2/8 ▶ Who has served as both the youngest and oldest American Defense Secretary?

> **A** Donald Rumsfeld **B** Leslie Aspin **C** Caspar Weinberger

2/9 ▶ In the Bible, what book immediately after Psalms also begins with P?

> **A** Book of Peter **B** Book of Prayers **C** Book of Proverbs

2/10 ▶ Which character sings 'Pure Imagination' in the stage musical *Charlie and the Chocolate Factory*?

> **A** Charlie Bucket **B** Willy Wonka **C** Grandpa Joe

2/11 ▶ Which of these words can be made from the chemical symbols of two noble gases?

> **A** Fear **B** Hear **C** Tear

2/12 ▶ Which band famously found popularity in Liverpool's Cavern Club?

> **A** The Beatles **B** The Dave Clark 5 **C** The Rolling Stones

QUIZ 2

Head to Head – The Beast Quiz 3

3/1 ▶ Usually removed and thrown away by cooks, what nickname is given to a long, pointed section of a crab's body?

> **A** Devil's toes **B** Dead man's fingers **C** Witch's hand

3/2 ▶ What was the population of the US at the time of its 2010 census?

> **A** 309 million **B** 409 million **C** 509 million

3/3 ▶ In the human body, inspiration and expiration are processes belonging to what system?

> **A** Respiratory System **B** Nervous System **C** Circulatory System

3/4 ▶ Which of these TV detectives was NOT based in California?

> **A** Jim Rockford **B** Columbo **C** Kojak

3/5 ▶ Which of these artists was principally a landscape watercolourist?

> **A** Turner **B** Gainsborough **C** Constable

3/6 ▶ What helicopter did Prince William fly as an RAF search and rescue captain?

> **A** Chinook **B** Apache **C** Sea King

3/7 ▶ Which of these words is spelled the same in English, French and German?

> **A** Police   **B** Mayor   **C** Taxi

3/8 ▶ In Greek myth, who saved the Argonauts from the music of the Sirens by playing his own more powerful music?

> **A** Bellerophon   **B** Orpheus   **C** Hector

3/9 ▶ On old maps of the world, the British Empire was traditionally marked by what colour?

> **A** Green   **B** Pink   **C** Blue

3/10 ▶ Katie White and Jules de Martino make up what musical duo?

> **A** Goldfrapp   **B** Hue and Cry   **C** The Ting Tings

3/11 ▶ Who is credited with popularising 'designer' jeans?

> **A** Calvin Klein   **B** Yves Saint Laurent   **C** Tommy Hilfiger

3/12 ▶ Which of these plays was the first to be performed on stage?

> **A** *Spring and Port Wine*   **B** *Suddenly Last Summer*   **C** *The Winter's Tale*

QUIZ 3

Head to Head – The Beast Quiz 4

4/1 ▶ Which is the largest of the terrestrial planets?

> **A** Earth   **B** Mars   **C** Venus

4/2 ▶ In 1939, which film was billed as 'The Greatest Picture in the History of Entertainment'?

> **A** *Gone with the Wind*   **B** *The Wizard of Oz*   **C** *Casablanca*

4/3 ▶ The French Cointreau family were manufacturers of what?

> **A** Biscuits   **B** Liqueur   **C** Chocolate

4/4 ▶ The five Kings of Scots between 1406 and 1542 all ruled under what name?

> **A** James   **B** Andrew   **C** Malcolm

4/5 ▶ Which of these occupations appears in the title of two novels by John Le Carré?

> **A** Tinker   **B** Tailor   **C** Soldier

4/6 ▶ Which brand of crisps takes its name from a variety of potato?

> **A** Walkers   **B** Golden Wonder   **C** McCoy's

4/7 ▷ Which of these bands did NOT feature on ITV's *The Big Reunion*?

> **A** Atomic Kitten **B** Liberty X **C** Big Fun

4/8 ▷ Which of these is the name of a finalist in the Women's 100 Metres at the 2013 Athletics World Championships?

> **A** English Gardner **B** German Carpinter **C** French Plummer

4/9 ▷ A pie chart is usually used in what branch of mathematics?

> **A** Algebra **B** Statistics **C** Calculus

4/10 ▷ In which city did John Lennon and Yoko Ono hold their first 'Bed-in for Peace' in 1969?

> **A** Amsterdam **B** Berlin **C** Paris

4/11 ▷ Which of these American Presidents was born furthest from the White House?

> **A** Barack Obama **B** John F Kennedy **C** Ronald Reagan

4/12 ▷ What was the nickname of King Harald I of Denmark?

> **A** Bluetooth **B** Broadband **C** Wifi

Head to Head – The Beast Quiz 5

5/1 ▶ In the film *The Night of the Lepus*, a region of Arizona is overrun by thousands of mutated, carnivorous killer what?

> **A** Sheep **B** Rabbits **C** Hedgehogs

5/2 ▶ Which of these countries is largest by area?

> **A** Guinea **B** Equatorial Guinea **C** Papua New Guinea

5/3 ▶ What type of dish is 'scouse'?

> **A** Fish soup **B** Cheese flan **C** Meat stew

5/4 ▶ Who designed Victoria Beckham's wedding dress?

> **A** Valentino **B** Vera Wang **C** Vivienne Westwood

5/5 ▶ Baseline to baseline, which of these playing courts is the longest?

> **A** Netball court **B** Volleyball court **C** Tennis court

5/6 ▶ The term 'tween' is used to describe people in what approximate age-range?

> **A** 3–6 **B** 8–14 **C** 18–21

5/7 ▶ Patricia Heaton played mother-of-three Debra Barone in what long-running US sitcom?

> **A** *Malcolm in the Middle* **B** *Everybody Loves Raymond*
> **C** *According to Jim*

5/8 ▶ Which mythical animal is a winged dragon with a barbed tail?

> **A** Gryphon   **B** Manticore   **C** Wyvern

5/9 ▶ In 2013, which J K Rowling character did David Cameron say he would most like to be?

> **A** Harry Potter   **B** Ron Weasley   **C** Severus Snape

5/10 ▶ Which Whitney Houston song was on the official soundtrack to the 1988 Olympics?

> **A** 'How Will I Know?'   **B** 'I Will Always Love You'   **C** 'One Moment In Time'

5/11 ▶ With almost 1,600 entries, what is the most frequently quoted work by Shakespeare in the *Oxford English Dictionary*?

> **A** *Romeo and Juliet*   **B** *Julius Caesar*   **C** *Hamlet*

5/12 ▶ Nearside neck shot and offside tail shot are terms in what sport?

> **A** Baseball   **B** Hurling   **C** Polo

QUIZ 5

Head to Head – The Beast Quiz 6

6/1 ▶ In which of these countries might you visit the Sahara desert?

> **A** Mali   **B** Malawi   **C** Mozambique

6/2 ▶ Cats are unlike most other mammals in that they can't taste what?

> **A** Sourness   **B** Sweetness   **C** Saltiness

6/3 ▶ Which of these is NOT a Jack Nicholson film?

> **A** *As Good As It Gets*   **B** *A Few Good Men*   **C** *Good Will Hunting*

6/4 ▶ Titoism was a form of communism practised in what country?

> **A** Czechoslovakia   **B** Soviet Union   **C** Yugoslavia

6/5 ▶ In the Gershwin musical *Porgy and Bess*, which character sings 'It Ain't Necessarily So'?

> **A** Sportin' Life   **B** Racin' Post   **C** Boxin' News

6/6 ▶ Which meat is a traditional ingredient in the dish Eggs Benedict?

> **A** Corned beef   **B** Ham   **C** Chicken

6/7 ▶ In the Swedish novel *Let the Right One In*, what mythical creature is the character Eli?

> **A** Mermaid   **B** Vampire   **C** Witch

6/8 ▶ Which ancient tribe once lived in what is now Switzerland?

> **A** Helvetii **B** Daci **C** Lusitani

6/9 ▶ James Brown's first UK hit single was 'Papa's got a Brand new...' what?

> **A** Bag **B** Wife **C** Hip

6/10 ▶ Which of these UK Saints' days is celebrated last in a calendar year?

> **A** St Andrew's Day **B** St George's Day **C** St Patrick's Day

6/11 ▶ Which of these is a centaur in the *Harry Potter* books?

> **A** Kian **B** Ronan **C** Shane

6/12 ▶ How is a plum duff traditionally cooked?

> **A** Baking **B** Poaching **C** Steaming

QUIZ 6

Head to Head – The Beast Quiz 7

7/1 ▷ What building is home to the London Philharmonic Orchestra?

> **A** Barbican Centre   **B** Royal College of Music   **C** Royal Festival Hall

7/2 ▷ Which South American country has won the most Miss World titles?

> **A** Brazil   **B** Peru   **C** Venezuela

7/3 ▷ Complete the saying: 'As rich as...'?

> **A** Midas   **B** Croesus   **C** Tantalus

7/4 ▷ In the TV series *The Six Million Dollar Man,* which of these parts of Steve Austin was NOT replaced by bionics?

> **A** His left eye   **B** His legs   **C** His right ear

7/5 ▷ The composer Berlioz was commonly known by what first name?

> **A** Harold   **B** Hector   **C** Horace

7/6 ▷ British Summer Time begins on the last Sunday in which month?

> **A** March   **B** April   **C** May

7/7 ▷ Which of these Bond films was released first?

> **A** *Die Another Day*   **B** *Live and Let Die*   **C** *Tomorrow Never Dies*

7/8 ▶ Which Prime Minister did Anthony Andrews play in *The King's Speech*?

> **A** Herbert Asquith **B** Stanley Baldwin **C** Winston Churchill

7/9 ▶ Which of these painters had a notorious lifelong feud with Sir Joshua Reynolds?

> **A** John Constable **B** Anthony van Dyck **C** Thomas Gainsborough

7/10 ▶ According to the TV theme song, which superhero was in 'satin tights, fighting for your rights'?

> **A** Captain America **B** Wonder Woman **C** Superman

7/11 ▶ Which of these elements is a solid at room temperature?

> **A** Boron **B** Radon **C** Xenon

7/12 ▶ What kind of foodstuff is a clingstone?

> **A** Cheese **B** Fruit **C** Nut

QUIZ 7

Head to Head – The Beast Quiz 8

8/1 ▶ How many Tests did the England cricket team win on the 2013–2014 tour of Australia?

A Four **B** Two **C** None

8/2 ▶ Which of these was a 16th-century female pirate?

A Grace Darling **B** Grace Helbig **C** Grace O'Malley

8/3 ▶ Which comedian is the author of the novels *The Secret Purposes* and *The Death of Eli Gold*?

A David Baddiel **B** Ben Elton **C** Mark Watson

8/4 ▶ What animal stands on the crown on the top of the Royal coat of arms?

A Lion **B** Owl **C** Unicorn

8/5 ▶ Which of these shapes does NOT have any lines of symmetry?

A Regular pentagon **B** Parallelogram **C** Rectangle

8/6 ▶ Which of these canals opened first?

A Panama Canal **B** Manchester Ship Canal **C** Suez Canal

8/7 ▶ *The X Factor* winner Sam Bailey's debut single was a cover version of which Demi Lovato song?

A 'Heart Attack' **B** 'La La Land' **C** 'Skyscraper'

HEAD-TO-HEAD QUESTIONS – THE BEAST

8/8 ▶ French President François Hollande is a member of which party?

> **A** Gaullist **B** Christian Democrat **C** Socialist

8/9 ▶ Stolen in Danny Boyle's 2013 art-heist film *Trance, Witches in the Air* is a work by which Spanish painter?

> **A** Goya **B** Murillo **C** Picasso

8/10 ▶ London's Fleet Street is named after what kind of geographical feature?

> **A** Hill **B** Wood **C** River

8/11 ▶ Which of these Welsh-born actors never won an Oscar?

> **A** Anthony Hopkins **B** Christian Bale **C** Richard Burton

8/12 ▶ Cancelled because of the war, both the 1940 Summer and Winter Olympics were scheduled to take place in what country?

> **A** Japan **B** Norway **C** US

Head to Head – The Beast Quiz 9

9/1 ▶ King Arthur is a character in what West End musical?

> **A** *The Book of Mormon*　**B** *Avenue Q*　**C** *Spamalot*

9/2 ▶ What is the oldest Scottish university?

> **A** St Andrews　**B** Edinburgh　**C** Heriot-Watt

9/3 ▶ On entering Downing Street for the first time in 1979, Margaret Thatcher quoted words attributed to which saint?

> **A** St George　**B** St Bernadette　**C** St Francis

9/4 ▶ How are the girls described in the title of a hit song for Queen?

> **A** Fat-bottomed　**B** Heavy-handed　**C** Big-boned

9/5 ▶ In which decade did Brazil win its first FIFA World Cup?

> **A** 1930s　**B** 1940s　**C** 1950s

9/6 ▶ In Greek myth, the Harpies' talons were made of what?

> **A** Bronze　**B** Gold　**C** Stone

9/7 ▶ What was the last century in which England and Wales did NOT have a queen as ruler?

> **A** 15th　**B** 16th　**C** 17th

9/8 ▶ Which *Harry Potter* character shares her first name with a star in the constellation of Orion?

> **A** Hermione Granger   **B** Minerva McGonagall   **C** Bellatrix Lestrange

9/9 ▶ Which TV show began 'Once upon a time there were three little girls who went to the police academy'?

> **A** *CATS Eyes*   **B** *Charlie's Angels*   **C** *Police Woman*

9/10 ▶ Tuna are members of the same family as which other fish?

> **A** Cod   **B** Mackerel   **C** Sardine

9/11 ▶ Which of these teams has never won cricket's County Championship?

> **A** Somerset   **B** Surrey   **C** Sussex

9/12 ▶ The 'sauna' bath originated in what country?

> **A** Finland   **B** Japan   **C** New Zealand

QUIZ 9

Head to Head – The Beast Quiz 10

10/1 ▶ The lovers in which E M Forster novel first meet in a Florence guest house?

> **A** *A Room with a View* **B** *Howards End* **C** *The Longest Journey*

10/2 ▶ Which infamous ruler was known as the 'Scourge of God'?

> **A** Ivan the Terrible **B** Genghis Khan **C** Attila the Hun

10/3 ▶ Impressionist Mike Yarwood created what catchphrase for Labour politician Denis Healey?

> **A** Tricky Dicky **B** Busy Lizzie **C** Silly Billy

10/4 ▶ Which of these is the name of a professional football player?

> **A** Patrick Darby **B** Liam Oakes **C** Sean St Ledger

10/5 ▶ According to *Billboard* magazine, who was the highest earning 'music money maker' of 2013?

> **A** Beyoncé **B** Madonna **C** Taylor Swift

10/6 ▶ Which of these superheroes was told to 'kneel before Zod!'?

> **A** Batman **B** Spider-Man **C** Superman

10/7 ▶ In the name of painter J M W Turner, what did the initial 'M' stand for?

> **A** Malachi **B** Mycroft **C** Mallord

10/8 ▶ In what language was the novel *One Hundred Years of Solitude* first published?

> **A** Spanish **B** Russian **C** Mandarin

10/9 ▶ Which of these fashion designers was first to release a perfume?

> **A** Giorgio Armani **B** Donna Karan **C** Coco Chanel

10/10 ▶ Which actress won two Golden Globes in 2007 for playing Elizabeth I and Elizabeth II?

> **A** Cate Blanchett **B** Helen Mirren **C** Miranda Richardson

10/11 ▶ What name is given to the medieval Danish confederation of Derby, Leicester, Lincoln, Nottingham and Stamford?

> **A** The Five Cities **B** The Five Towns **C** The Five Boroughs

10/12 ▶ In the words of a 1978 UK Number One single, which artist 'painted Salford's smoky tops'?

> **A** John Constable **B** L S Lowry **C** Joshua Reynolds

QUIZ 10

HEAD TO HEAD WITH

The
SINNERMAN

Head to Head – The Sinnerman Quiz 1

1/1 ▶ Which of these women was Queen of both England and France?

> **A** Catherine of Aragon   **B** Eleanor of Aquitaine   **C** Helen of Troy

1/2 ▶ How is the number ten expressed in binary notation?

> **A** 10   **B** 1010   **C** 110

1/3 ▶ Who said 'It's hard to be humble when you're as great as I am'?

> **A** Muhammad Ali   **B** George W Bush   **C** Justin Bieber

1/4 ▶ What is the first novel in George R R Martin's series *A Song of Ice and Fire*?

> **A** *A Clash of Kings*   **B** *A Feast for Crows*   **C** *A Game of Thrones*

1/5 ▶ What Scottish port is known as the 'Gateway to the Isles'?

> **A** Ullapool   **B** Ballantrae   **C** Oban

1/6 ▶ Which of these names is NOT associated with the Eurovision Song Contest?

> **A** Paul Hogan   **B** Johnny Logan   **C** Terry Wogan

1/7 ▶ A Formula One race, if not suspended, must end after how many hours?

> **A** One   **B** Two   **C** Three

1/8 ▷ In maths, an obelus is a sign to indicate what?

> **A** Addition   **B** Division   **C** Multiplication

1/9 ▷ Which fictional car is described in song as 'Our fine four fendered friend'?

> **A** Chitty Chitty Bang Bang   **B** Genevieve   **C** Herbie

1/10 ▷ Which of these battles took place most recently?

> **A** Bosworth Field   **B** Marston Moor   **C** Hastings

1/11 ▷ In 2013, who became the first member of the Royal Family to open a Twitter account?

> **A** Duke of York   **B** Earl of Wessex   **C** Princess Royal

1/12 ▷ Traditional croissants are what shape?

> **A** Crescent   **B** Ring   **C** Dome

QUIZ 1

Head to Head – The Sinnerman Quiz 2

2/1 ▶ The Bass Strait separates Tasmania from what mainland Australian state?

> **A** New South Wales   **B** Queensland   **C** Victoria

2/2 ▶ In biology, what is the smallest unit capable of independent existence?

> **A** Atom   **B** Cell   **C** Nucleus

2/3 ▶ Which of these letters is NOT used in the system of Roman numerals?

> **A** D   **B** M   **C** E

2/4 ▶ The small bones found in human fingers and toes are called the what?

> **A** Carpals   **B** Phalanges   **C** Patellas

2/5 ▶ Backed by 'The Starlettes', which astrologer released the novelty single 'No Matter What Sign You Are'?

> **A** Jonathan Cainer   **B** Russell Grant   **C** Mystic Meg

2/6 ▶ Which of these films was released the earliest?

> **A** *Antz*   **B** *A Bug's Life*   **C** *The Fly*

2/7 ▶ Two-digit numbers ending with which of these cannot be prime numbers?

> **A** 5   **B** 7   **C** 9

2/8 ▶ Which of these is the name of a vascular network at the base of the brain?

> **A** Circle of Willis   **B** Loop of Clooney   **C** Star of Gibson

2/9 ▶ At which of these would you be most likely to see 'tic-tac' being used for communication?

> **A** Royal Ascot   **B** Royal Albert Hall   **C** Royal Academy

2/10 ▶ In a song from *Winnie-the-Pooh*, Tigger says his bottom is made out of what?

> **A** Rubber   **B** Springs   **C** Blubber

2/11 ▶ Which group of elements is the furthest right on the periodic table?

> **A** Noble Gases   **B** Transition Metals   **C** Alkali Metals

2/12 ▶ Which of these novels was NOT originally published in Russian?

> **A** *Crime and Punishment*   **B** *Sense and Sensibility*   **C** *War and Peace*

QUIZ 2

Head to Head – The Sinnerman Quiz 3

3/1 ▶ When mourning a cat, ancient Egyptians were said to shave their what?

> **A** Legs   **B** Armpits   **C** Eyebrows

3/2 ▶ Which of these music stars was knighted first?

> **A** Paul McCartney   **B** Elton John   **C** Cliff Richard

3/3 ▶ Who are the rulers in a stratocracy?

> **A** The clergy   **B** The military   **C** The working classes

3/4 ▶ Men of which of these nationalities have NOT been manager of the England football team?

> **A** French   **B** Italian   **C** Swedish

3/5 ▶ Launched in 1964, which fashion retailer began in the basement of the former department chain, Peter Robinson Ltd?

> **A** Evans   **B** River Island   **C** Topshop

3/6 ▶ In the musical *Little Shop of Horrors*, what's the occupation of Orin Scrivello, Audrey's boyfriend?

> **A** Vet   **B** Dentist   **C** Doctor

3/7 ▶ The name of what meat also means to have a grievance with someone?

> **A** Beef   **B** Pork   **C** Goose

3/8 ▶ Who played the Divination teacher Professor Trelawney in the *Harry Potter* films?

> **A** Emma Thompson   **B** Miriam Margoyles   **C** Zoë Wanamaker

3/9 ▶ Born in Scotland, Sir Eduardo Paolozzi worked mostly as what type of artist?

> **A** Portrait painter   **B** Sculptor   **C** Textile artist

3/10 ▶ What name did The Goodies give to their martial art, which used black puddings as weapons?

> **A** Ee By Gum   **B** Ecky Thump   **C** Is It Eck As Like

3/11 ▶ The author who created Moll Flanders also created which other famous fictional character?

> **A** Robinson Crusoe   **B** Bilbo Baggins   **C** Tom Sawyer

3/12 ▶ 'Come and Get It' was a 2013 Top 10 hit for which former teen star?

> **A** Selena Gomez   **B** Demi Lovato   **C** Miley Cyrus

QUIZ 3

Head to Head – The Sinnerman Quiz 4

4/1 ▶ Which of these explorers was NOT born in Portugal?

> **A** Ferdinand Magellan   **B** Marco Polo   **C** Vasco da Gama

4/2 ▶ Alex Ferguson was in charge of Manchester United for how many games?

> **A** 1,000   **B** 1,500   **C** 2,000

4/3 ▶ Which American actress married Hugh Dancy in 2009?

> **A** Claire Danes   **B** Katherine Heigl   **C** Kirsten Dunst

4/4 ▶ What is the final book in the *Twilight Saga*?

> **A** *Breaking Dawn*   **B** *New Moon*   **C** *Eclipse*

4/5 ▶ In 2005 Caroline of Hanover became the heir to which country's throne?

> **A** Liechtenstein   **B** Luxembourg   **C** Monaco

4/6 ▶ Which of these is the name of a variety of apple?

> **A** Naseby White   **B** Balaclava Yellow   **C** Blenheim Orange

4/7 ▶ China claims ownership of the entire world population of which animal?

> **A** South China Tiger   **B** Giant Panda   **C** Large Bamboo Rat

4/8 ▶ Which of these countries does NOT use a currency called the Krona?

> **A** Sweden   **B** Finland   **C** Iceland

4/9 ▶ What is the sixth planet from the Sun?

> **A** Mars   **B** Saturn   **C** Uranus

4/10 ▶ What song title is shared by Number Ones for Lisa Stansfield and Oasis?

> **A** 'All Around the World'   **B** 'Change'   **C** 'Some Might Say'

4/11 ▶ Which of these is NOT a David Beckham men's fragrance?

> **A** Instinct   **B** Intimately   **C** Infectious

4/12 ▶ What is the largest country that the Tropic of Capricorn passes through?

> **A** Brazil   **B** India   **C** Australia

QUIZ 4

Head to Head – The Sinnerman Quiz 5

5/1 ▶ A 'saucière' is another name for what?

> **A** Gravy boat   **B** Toast Rack   **C** Saucer

5/2 ▶ In 2013, who became the first American to have seven consecutive Number One albums in the UK?

> **A** Eminem   **B** Jay-Z   **C** Usher

5/3 ▶ The vicuña is the smallest member of what family of animals?

> **A** Camelidae   **B** Equidae   **C** Bovidae

5/4 ▶ Which Will Smith film has the tagline 'The last man on Earth is not alone'?

> **A** *Independence Day*   **B** *Men in Black*   **C** *I Am Legend*

5/5 ▶ Boucles d'or is the French name of what fairy tale character?

> **A** Goldilocks   **B** Red Riding Hood   **C** Snow White

5/6 ▶ Which of these is NOT the name of an activity-related injury?

> **A** Climber's finger   **B** Fencer's thumb   **C** Tennis Elbow

5/7 ▶ Which of these peoples invaded the British Isles most recently?

> **A** Anglo-Saxons   **B** Normans   **C** Vikings

HEAD-TO-HEAD QUESTIONS – THE SINNERMAN

5/8 ▶ The wedding dress belonging to which of these women sold at auction for over £121,000 in 2013?

> **A** Yoko Ono   **B** Bianca Jagger   **C** Elizabeth Taylor

5/9 ▶ Which of these songs was a Number One hit for Beyoncé most recently?

> **A** 'Crazy in Love'   **B** 'Déjà Vu'   **C** 'If I Were a Boy'

5/10 ▶ What was the operational codename of the 1943 'Dambusters' raid?

> **A** Compass   **B** Crossbow   **C** Chastise

5/11 ▶ Richard Blackwood played Donkey in the West End production of what musical?

> **A** *Shrek*   **B** *The Lion King*   **C** *Wicked*

5/12 ▶ Thomas Jefferson claimed the role of which profession was 'to question everything, yield nothing, and talk by the hour'?

> **A** Doctors   **B** Lawyers   **C** Plumbers

QUIZ 5

Head to Head – The Sinnerman Quiz 6

6/1 ▷ In Greek mythology, the gods had 'ichor' instead of what?

> **A** Blood   **B** Sweat   **C** Tears

6/2 ▷ The ferret belongs to what animal family?

> **A** Weasel   **B** Cat   **C** Mouse

6/3 ▷ Who won an Oscar for playing a Country and Western singer in the film *Tender Mercies*?

> **A** Jeff Bridges   **B** Robert Duvall   **C** Sissy Spacek

6/4 ▷ What did Edward III do with the Crown Jewels during his reign?

> **A** Broke them up   **B** Lost them   **C** Pawned them

6/5 ▷ When commenting on tax, which comedian claimed 'I invented self-assessment'?

> **A** Ken Dodd   **B** Jasper Carrott   **C** Frankie Boyle

6/6 ▷ In the 1970s, who became the first woman to have a solo UK Number One hit with a self-written song?

> **A** Tina Charles   **B** Julie Covington   **C** Kate Bush

HEAD-TO-HEAD QUESTIONS – THE SINNERMAN

6/7 ▶ What is the national currency in Serbia?

> **A** Dinar **B** Tolar **C** Euro

6/8 ▶ The creator of which long-running TV quiz was inspired by his experiences as a prisoner of war in Germany?

> **A** *Mastermind* **B** *Fifteen to One* **C** *Weakest Link*

6/9 ▶ Which of these famous people were born first?

> **A** Grandma Moses **B** Mama Cass **C** Papa Doc Duvalier

6/10 ▶ After the capital Riyadh, what is Saudi Arabia's second most populous city?

> **A** Mecca **B** Medina **C** Jeddah

6/11 ▶ 'I love you, but we only have 14 hours to save the Earth!' is a line from what film?

> **A** *Star Wars* **B** *Flash Gordon* **C** *Armageddon*

6/12 ▶ In the human body, the spleen is part of what system?

> **A** Circulatory **B** Digestive **C** Lymphatic

Head to Head – The Sinnerman Quiz 7

7/1 ▷ Which of these countries is NOT a setting for a Bizet opera?

> **A** Spain **B** Ceylon **C** Switzerland

7/2 ▷ A situation where it is difficult to tell which of two things existed first is called what?

> **A** Bacon and egg problem **B** Egg and spoon problem
> **C** Chicken and egg problem

7/3 ▷ Which Take That singer performed a duet with Agnetha Fältskog on her 2013 album?

> **A** Gary Barlow **B** Mark Owen **C** Robbie Williams

7/4 ▷ Which of these footballers captained England the most times?

> **A** Alan Shearer **B** Emlyn Hughes **C** Tony Adams

7/5 ▷ Which of these continents was NOT the location of any of the Seven Wonders of the Ancient World?

> **A** Asia **B** Europe **C** South America

7/6 ▷ Practised by Sylvester Stallone's mother Jackie, telling fortunes by reading someone's backside is called what?

> **A** Rumpology **B** Tushology **C** Buttology

HEAD-TO-HEAD QUESTIONS – THE SINNERMAN

7/7 ▶ In 1984, the character Jack Ryan was introduced in what book?

A *The Sum of All Fears* **B** *Patriot Games* **C** *The Hunt for Red October*

7/8 ▶ Which of these is a slang term meaning 'very happy' or 'excited'?

A Cambridged **B** Newcastled **C** Stoked

7/9 ▶ A tangelo is a hybrid of a tangerine and what other fruit?

A Lemon **B** Grapefruit **C** Lime

7/10 ▶ The actor Steve McQueen had his first lead role in which 1958 film?

A *The Blob* **B** *The Thing* **C** *The Fly*

7/11 ▶ Great Britain won silver and bronze in what sport at the 2014 Winter Olympics?

A Curling **B** Freestyle Skiing **C** Ice dancing

7/12 ▶ Lady Gaga has NOT worn fashion items made out of which of these?

A Raw meat **B** Razor blades **C** Kermit the Frog

Head to Head – The Sinnerman Quiz 8

8/1 ▶ 'Anserine', meaning 'goose-like', is also used to describe someone who is what?

> **A** Flighty **B** Noisy **C** Silly

8/2 ▶ Which film director said 'There is no terror in a bang, only the anticipation of it'?

> **A** Steven Spielberg **B** Alfred Hitchcock **C** George A Romero

8/3 ▶ Alvin Hall is a TV and radio expert in what area?

> **A** Food **B** Fashion **C** Finance

8/4 ▶ Which ballerina was born Edris Stannus in Ireland in 1898?

> **A** Ninette de Valois **B** Alicia Markova **C** Margot Fonteyn

8/5 ▶ Which of these is the name of a retired tennis player?

> **A** Anna Lobnova **B** Anna Smashnova **C** Anna Volinova

8/6 ▶ In the Lucian Freud painting *Eli and David*, what animal is Eli?

> **A** Rabbit **B** Cat **C** Dog

8/7 ▶ Played on board ships, the objects thrown in a game of deck quoits are usually made from what?

> **A** Stone **B** Rope **C** Glass

8/8 ▶ Which of these actors has NOT played Superman on the big screen?

> **A** Brandon Routh **B** Henry Cavill **C** Jeremy Renner

8/9 ▶ Jules Verne's *Journey to the Centre of the Earth* begins at a volcano in what country?

> **A** Iceland **B** Indonesia **C** Italy

8/10 ▶ Which of these instruments measures wind speed?

> **A** Barometer **B** Hygrometer **C** Anemometer

8/11 ▶ Which of these is an alternative name for the oceanic bonito?

> **A** Potato cod **B** Rainbow trout **C** Skipjack tuna

8/12 ▶ In Greek myth, what group of goddesses were also known as the Charites?

> **A** Gorgons **B** Muses **C** Graces

QUIZ 8

Head to Head – The Sinnerman Quiz 9

9/1 ▶ Which character in a Tim Burton film is summoned if you say his name three times?

> **A** Beetlejuice   **B** Frankenweenie   **C** Willy Wonka

9/2 ▶ Hunter S Thompson claimed which president 'could shake your hand and stab you in the back at the same time'?

> **A** Richard Nixon   **B** Ronald Reagan   **C** Bill Clinton

9/3 ▶ Which of these Dickens novels was written first?

> **A** *Martin Chuzzlewit*   **B** *David Copperfield*   **C** *Oliver Twist*

9/4 ▶ In 2014, *So Long, See You Tomorrow* became the first UK Number One album for what band?

> **A** Agra Aeroplane Club   **B** Bombay Bicycle Club   **C** Calcutta Coach Club

9/5 ▶ The Three Shire Stone in the Lake District is where Cumberland, Westmorland and which other county once met?

> **A** Yorkshire   **B** Lancashire   **C** Durham

9/6 ▶ Which of these has an alkaline rather than acidic sting?

> **A** Bumblebee   **B** Stinging Nettle   **C** Wasp

HEAD-TO-HEAD QUESTIONS – THE SINNERMAN

9/7 ▶ What is singer Mike Rosenberg's stage name?

> **A** Passenger **B** Traveller **C** Commuter

9/8 ▶ The International Bible Students Association developed into which religious group?

> **A** Quakers **B** Jehovah's Witnesses **C** Salvation Army

9/9 ▶ Which of these English astronomers was a pioneer of photography?

> **A** Edmond Halley **B** John Herschel **C** Fred Hoyle

9/10 ▶ The Peabody Hotel in Memphis, Tennessee is noted for the twice-daily walk through the lobby by which animals?

> **A** Chimpanzees **B** Ducks **C** Pygmy goats

9/11 ▶ Which Prime Minister succeeded his wife's uncle?

> **A** Herbert Asquith **B** Neville Chamberlain **C** Anthony Eden

9/12 ▶ At over 7 metres in length, what is the longest species of snake?

> **A** Bevel-nosed boa **B** Palm viper **C** Reticulated python

QUIZ 9

Head to Head – The Sinnerman Quiz 10

10/1 ▶ Which of these athletes never won an Olympic Gold medal?

> **A** Colin Jackson **B** Jonathan Edwards **C** Linford Christie

10/2 ▶ What city in Morocco held international status until 1956?

> **A** Agadir **B** Fez **C** Tangier

10/3 ▶ Where would you find a barrier known as a groyne?

> **A** On a beach **B** Up a mountain **C** Down a mine

10/4 ▶ Which scientist wrote the book known as *The Voyage of the Beagle*?

> **A** Charles Darwin **B** Isaac Newton **C** Michael Faraday

10/5 ▶ What is the maximum age a cardinal can vote for a new pope?

> **A** 79 **B** 89 **C** 99

10/6 ▶ Which of these cathedrals owns an original copy of the Magna Carta?

> **A** Bury St Edmunds **B** Guildford **C** Lincoln

10/7 ▶ Cardinal Wolsey is a character in which *Carry On* film?

> **A** *Carry On Jack* **B** *Carry On Henry* **C** *Carry On Dick*

10/8 ▷ Which of these Grand National fences is jumped first?

> **A** Canal Turn   **B** Valentine's Brook   **C** Becher's Brook

10/9 ▷ The dish *spaghetti aglio e olio* consists of pasta served with what?

> **A** Tomato and basil   **B** Chicken and mushroom   **C** Garlic and oil

10/10 ▷ Which person, who has a dog breed named after him, was called 'The Sporting Parson'?

> **A** Dandie Dinmont   **B** Jack Russell   **C** St Bernard

10/11 ▷ On 1960s TV, what was the name of *The Girl from U.N.C.L.E.*?

> **A** April Dancer   **B** May Prancer   **C** June Rudolph

10/12 ▷ The country of Montenegro has its coastline on which sea?

> **A** Adriatic   **B** Baltic   **C** Aegean

QUIZ 10

HEAD TO HEAD WITH

The

BARRISTER

Head to Head – The Barrister Quiz 1

1/1 ▶ 'Sorry we're closed' was the last line in what long-running US sitcom?

> **A** *Cheers*　**B** *Friends*　**C** *Frasier*

1/2 ▶ Which of these musicals by Andrew Lloyd Webber premiered first?

> **A** *Aspects of Love*　**B** *Cats*　**C** *Evita*

1/3 ▶ What's the collective noun for a group of rhinos?

> **A** Crash　**B** Bang　**C** Wallop

1/4 ▶ Which team was beaten by the US at the 1950 FIFA World Cup in the huge upset known as the 'Miracle on Grass'?

> **A** Brazil　**B** England　**C** Italy

1/5 ▶ Prince George of Cambridge was christened in which palace?

> **A** St James's Palace　**B** Buckingham Palace　**C** Kensington Palace

1/6 ▶ Before his birth, which Biblical hero's mother was visited by an angel who said 'No razor shall come on his head'?

> **A** Joshua　**B** Moses　**C** Samson

1/7 ▶ Beans and spicy sausages are the main ingredients of what Spanish dish?

> **A** Tortilla española   **B** Fabada   **C** Gazpacho

1/8 ▶ Which of these American presidents served two terms?

> **A** Hoover   **B** Eisenhower   **C** Ford

1/9 ▶ 'Horrorscope' and 'designer genes' are examples of which figure of speech?

> **A** Euphemism   **B** Hyperbole   **C** Pun

1/10 ▶ Which of these songs was a hit earliest for The Beatles?

> **A** 'Help!'   **B** 'Hello Goodbye'   **C** 'Hey Jude'

1/11 ▶ Which spirit is added to Dubonnet to make a Dubonnet Cocktail?

> **A** Cognac   **B** Vodka   **C** Gin

1/12 ▶ What type of lightning is usually formed by a cloud-to-ground discharge?

> **A** Sheet   **B** Forked   **C** Ball

QUIZ 1

Head to Head – The Barrister Quiz 2

2/1 ▶ In which of these sports was Hawk-Eye used first?

> **A** Polo   **B** Cricket   **C** Tennis

2/2 ▶ Which of these countries does NOT have a coastline on the Caspian Sea?

> **A** Iran   **B** Turkmenistan   **C** Uzbekistan

2/3 ▶ What is the title of the 2013 spin-off of the animated Disney film *Cars*?

> **A** Trains   **B** Planes   **C** Boats

2/4 ▶ Who wrote the novel *The Good Companions*?

> **A** J B Priestley   **B** J D Salinger   **C** J M Coetzee

2/5 ▶ Which of these animals is classified as a rodent?

> **A** Pangolin   **B** Porcupine   **C** Platypus

2/6 ▶ Which of these groups had a US Number One single before the others?

> **A** The Dave Clark Five   **B** The Jackson 5   **C** Maroon 5

2/7 ▶ Which of these pronouns is also a symbol for a chemical element?

> **A** He   **B** Me   **C** We

HEAD-TO-HEAD QUESTIONS – THE BARRISTER

2/8 ▷ Which of these is NOT a fictional TV football team?

> **A** Emmerdale Albion   **B** Walford Town   **C** Weatherfield County

2/9 ▷ In France, what dessert is known as an *omelette à la norvégienne*, which translates as 'Norwegian omelette'?

> **A** Trifle   **B** Baked Alaska   **C** Pavlova

2/10 ▷ What phrase did Julius Caesar supposedly utter when crossing the Rubicon and initiating a Roman civil war?

> **A** 'The die is cast'   **B** 'And you, Brutus?'   **C** 'I came, I saw, I conquered'

2/11 ▷ What was the first Summer Olympics NOT held in a capital city?

> **A** Antwerp   **B** Melbourne   **C** St Louis

2/12 ▷ In the 2008 Christmas chart, which song appeared three times by three different artists?

> **A** 'Hallelujah'   **B** 'A Moment Like This'   **C** 'That's My Goal'

Head to Head – The Barrister Quiz 3

3/1 ▶ Which TV presenter gained her pilot's licence in 2013?

> **A** Carol Vorderman **B** Kate Humble **C** Alex Jones

3/2 ▶ What celestial objects are largely composed of ice?

> **A** Asteroids **B** Comets **C** Meteorites

3/3 ▶ Which retired heavyweight boxing champion co-wrote the spiritual memoir *The Soul of a Butterfly*?

> **A** Muhammad Ali **B** Lennox Lewis **C** Mike Tyson

3/4 ▶ What shade is the traditional colour for a Buddhist monk's robe?

> **A** Puce **B** Saffron **C** Teal

3/5 ▶ Which of these singers is the youngest?

> **A** Conor Maynard **B** Harry Styles **C** Justin Bieber

3/6 ▶ What is the value of the bet offered to Phileas Fogg in the Jules Verne novel *Around the World in 80 Days*?

> **A** £20,000 **B** £50,000 **C** £100,000

HEAD-TO-HEAD QUESTIONS – THE BARRISTER

3/7 ▶ Which of these professionals would be most likely to wear 'scrubs'?

> **A** Prison officer   **B** Cleaner   **C** Surgeon

3/8 ▶ 'Cat's paw' and 'monkey's fist' are types of what?

> **A** Knot   **B** Hairstyle   **C** Dance move

3/9 ▶ Which of these bands was the first to have a UK Top 10 hit?

> **A** Heaven 17   **B** Level 42   **C** UB40

3/10 ▶ At the 2012 London Olympics, Tom Daley won which colour medal?

> **A** Bronze   **B** Silver   **C** Gold

3/11 ▶ Which of these is NOT an official language of the United Nations?

> **A** German   **B** Arabic   **C** Russian

3/12 ▶ Which Scottish National Park is the largest in Britain?

> **A** Cairngorms   **B** Loch Lomond   **C** Grampians

Head to Head – The Barrister Quiz 4

4/1 ▶ What caused future US President Franklin Roosevelt to have to use a wheelchair from 1921 onwards?

> **A** Sports accident   **B** Gunshot wound   **C** Polio

4/2 ▶ Which of these girls' names does NOT appear in Lou Bega's 'Mambo No. 5'?

> **A** Jessica   **B** Monica   **C** Amanda

4/3 ▶ Where are the Descartes Formation and the Cayley Formation located?

> **A** Antarctica   **B** Pacific Ocean seabed   **C** The Moon

4/4 ▶ What is the name of the unique number that every UK police officer is issued with at the date of their joining?

> **A** Commission number   **B** Pledge number   **C** Warrant number

4/5 ▶ Which Tretchikoff painting is thought to be the world's most reproduced print?

> **A** *Chinese Girl*   **B** *Balinese Girl*   **C** *Swazi Girl*

4/6 ▶ The 1696 tax that was only repealed in 1851 was on what?

> **A** Coffee   **B** Silk   **C** Windows

4/7 ▶ The coccygeus muscle is found in what part of the body?

> **A** Foot   **B** Lower back   **C** Neck

4/8 ▶ Which of these is the title of Gillian Flynn's novel about the disappearance of Amy Dunne on her fifth wedding anniversary?

> **A** *Gone Girl*   **B** *Missing Mummy*   **C** *Woman Withdrawn*

4/9 ▶ What is the only American state whose name can be typed on one row of a QWERTY keyboard?

> **A** Alaska   **B** Maine   **C** Ohio

4/10 ▶ In the musical *The King and I* what was the first name of 'I'?

> **A** Agatha   **B** Alice   **C** Anna

4/11 ▶ In Greek myth what animals pulled Achilles' chariot?

> **A** Dogs   **B** Horses   **C** Snakes

4/12 ▶ Which of these was created in 1903 by Alfred Harmsworth as 'a newspaper for women, run by women'?

> **A** Daily Mirror   **B** Daily Express   **C** Daily Star

QUIZ 4

Head to Head – The Barrister Quiz 5

5/1 ▶ Which of these birds does NOT appear in the name of a London train station?

> **A** Canary **B** Heron **C** Penguin

5/2 ▶ 'Tablet' is a hard Scottish form of what confection?

> **A** Fudge **B** Marzipan **C** Nougat

5/3 ▶ In what game does someone give the initial of a famous person and the other players have to guess who it is?

> **A** Botticelli **B** Canaletto **C** Giotto

5/4 ▶ Which of these African countries is a setting in a Shakespeare play?

> **A** Algeria **B** Egypt **C** Tunisia

5/5 ▶ What term describes the side of a ship that is turned away from the wind?

> **A** Leeward **B** Landward **C** Leftward

5/6 ▶ What name is given to the point in the celestial sphere directly 'above' an observer?

> **A** Zenith **B** Nadir **C** Azimuth

5/7 ▶ What spice was once called Indian saffron because of its orange-yellow colour?

> **A** Cardamom **B** Nutmeg **C** Turmeric

5/8 ▶ What Second World War gun, manufactured in Enfield, was invented by Major R V Shepherd and H J Turpin?

A Sten gun   **B** Bren gun   **C** Tommy gun

5/9 ▶ Why was Madonna banned from returning to an American cinema chain in 2013?

A Bringing her own food   **B** Throwing popcorn   **C** Texting

5/10 ▶ Who was the only person to both score and be booked in the 1966 World Cup Final?

A Geoff Hurst   **B** Wolfgang Weber   **C** Martin Peters

5/11 ▶ The giant naked figure sculpted into the chalk hillside above Cerne Abbas is holding what in his hand?

A Club   **B** Olive branch   **C** Tankard

5/12 ▶ With three inhabitants per square kilometre, what is the most sparsely populated country in Europe?

A Belarus   **B** Iceland   **C** Albania

QUIZ 5

Head to Head – The Barrister Quiz 6

6/1 ▶ What TV series and film was inspired by the real-life case of Doctor Sam Sheppard?

A *The Fugitive* **B** *The Singing Detective* **C** *The Untouchables*

6/2 ▶ The British company Rough Trade is involved in what industry?

A Music **B** Outdoor clothing **C** Weapons

6/3 ▶ Played on film by Laurence Olivier, which Roman general put down the slave revolt led by Spartacus?

A Pompey **B** Julius Caesar **C** Crassus

6/4 ▶ Novelist Harper Lee worked as an assistant to Truman Capote on what book?

A *Breakfast at Tiffany's* **B** *In Cold Blood* **C** *The Grass Harp*

6/5 ▶ In the run-up to Lent, Collop Monday was a day for getting rid of what food?

A Fish **B** Meat **C** Potatoes

6/6 ▶ Alongside his parliamentary duties, Black Rod is the principal usher of what order of chivalry?

A Order of the Garter **B** Order of the Bath **C** Order of the Thistle

6/7 ▶ Cavolo nero is a variety of what?

> **A** Cabbage **B** Mushroom **C** Grape

6/8 ▶ Which Bond actor appeared in the film *Mrs Doubtfire*?

> **A** Daniel Craig **B** George Lazenby **C** Pierce Brosnan

6/9 ▶ Which of these dances is the oldest?

> **A** Foxtrot **B** Polka **C** Jive

6/10 ▶ British writer Conn Iggulden is a bestselling author in what genre?

> **A** Historical fiction **B** Fantasy **C** Crime thriller

6/11 ▶ In music, a rhythm altered to stress the 'off-beats' is known as what?

> **A** Singularization **B** Syncopation **C** Synchronization

6/12 ▶ Which of these is a medical condition?

> **A** Alien ear syndrome **B** Alien hand syndrome
> **C** Alien foot syndrome

QUIZ 6

Head to Head – The Barrister Quiz 7

7/1 ▶ A line from Shakespeare's *Antony and Cleopatra* is 'In time we hate that which we often...' what?

> **A** Love   **B** Fear   **C** Ignore

7/2 ▶ What single work of art is created by a group of images relating to each other in some way?

> **A** Montage   **B** Motif   **C** Mezzotint

7/3 ▶ Matthew Webb used what stroke when becoming the first man to swim the Channel?

> **A** Breaststroke   **B** Front crawl   **C** Backstroke

7/4 ▶ Carnauba wax comes from what part of the Brazilian palm tree?

> **A** Bark   **B** Leaf   **C** Root

7/5 ▶ Which of these is NOT a TV cookery programme featuring Jamie Oliver?

> **A** *15-Minute Meals*   **B** *30-Minute Meals*   **C** *60-Minute Meals*

7/6 ▶ The yellowhammer belongs to which family of birds?

> **A** Bunting   **B** Cuckoo   **C** Lark

7/7 ▷ Which of the Earth's layers is thought to be broken up into tectonic plates?

> **A** Lithosphere   **B** Biosphere   **C** Troposphere

7/8 ▷ Which of these songs was a hit the earliest?

> **A** 'Morning Has Broken'   **B** 'Afternoon Delight'   **C** 'Night Fever'

7/9 ▷ When the AGA cooker was invented in the 1920s, what was the original fuel used?

> **A** Wood   **B** Oil   **C** Coal

7/10 ▷ With reference to wine, what does the word *chambré* mean?

> **A** Corked   **B** Aged   **C** At room temperature

7/11 ▷ The macula lutea is part of which sensory organ?

> **A** Eye   **B** Ear   **C** Nose

7/12 ▷ Which actor claimed to have been born Taidje Khan on the Russian island of Sakhalin?

> **A** Yul Brynner   **B** Charles Bronson   **C** Ernest Borgnine

QUIZ 7

Head to Head – The Barrister Quiz 8

8/1 ▶ The books *El Clásico* and *Fear and Loathing in La Liga* are both about the rivalry between which two football teams?

A Juventus & AC Milan   **B** Porto & Benfica   **C** Real Madrid & Barcelona

8/2 ▶ In 'The Twelve Days of Christmas', which of these are there most of?

A Calling birds   **B** Laying geese   **C** Swimming swans

8/3 ▶ What surname links the second and sixth US Presidents?

A Adams   **B** Johnson   **C** Roosevelt

8/4 ▶ Which motorway connects London and Bristol?

A M2   **B** M4   **C** M6

8/5 ▶ Which of these American TV shows was NOT a spin-off?

A *Mork and Mindy*   **B** *The Bionic Woman*   **C** *Falcon Crest*

8/6 ▶ Members of the Gerridae family of insects are called 'Jesus bugs' because of their ability to do what?

A Come back to life   **B** Walk on water   **C** Cure leprosy

HEAD-TO-HEAD QUESTIONS – THE BARRISTER

8/7 ▶ Which of these is a suburb of North London?

> **A** Southgate   **B** Southwold   **C** Southport

8/8 ▶ What nickname was given to Lindow Man, the Iron Age body found in a Cheshire bog in 1984?

> **A** Mac Elsfield   **B** Pete Marsh   **C** Nan Twitch

8/9 ▶ Which Labour Prime Minister became Viscount Prestwood?

> **A** Clement Attlee   **B** Harold Wilson   **C** James Callaghan

8/10 ▶ Which director said 'My doctor told me to stop having intimate dinners for four, unless there are three other people'?

> **A** Quentin Tarantino   **B** David Fincher   **C** Orson Welles

8/11 ▶ Boxer Sugar Ray Robinson was five time world champion in what weight division?

> **A** Heavyweight   **B** Middleweight   **C** Lightweight

8/12 ▶ Which of these African countries is NOT a kingdom?

> **A** Lesotho   **B** Malawi   **C** Swaziland

QUIZ 8

Head to Head – The Barrister Quiz 9

9/1 ▶ Which cartoon couple got married at Shotgun Pete's Wedding Chapel?

> **A** Fred and Wilma Flintstone   **B** Homer and Marge Simpson
> **C** George and Jane Jetson

9/2 ▶ Grits, a common breakfast dish in the US, most closely resembles which of these?

> **A** Porridge   **B** Pancakes   **C** Black pudding

9/3 ▶ The mummy of which pharaoh was issued with a passport when he was flown to France for restoration in 1976?

> **A** Khufu   **B** Tutankhamun   **C** Rameses II

9/4 ▶ Which of these bones is found in the leg?

> **A** Sternum   **B** Tibia   **C** Ulna

9/5 ▶ LaTavia Roberson and LeToya Luckett were original members of which girl group?

> **A** Destiny's Child   **B** Eternal   **C** En Vogue

9/6 ▶ In Roman mythology, which god was the father of Jupiter?

> **A** Mars   **B** Neptune   **C** Saturn

9/7 ▶ Which flavour liqueur combines with vodka and cream to make a White Russian cocktail?

> **A** Coffee **B** Chocolate **C** Orange

9/8 ▶ In Ernest Hemingway's book *The Old Man and the Sea,* the title character catches a magnificent example of which fish?

> **A** Tuna **B** Marlin **C** Shark

9/9 ▶ Which of these countries has a population of over one million?

> **A** Maldives **B** Malta **C** Mauritius

9/10 ▶ Lord Liverpool is the only British Prime Minister to accede to office as a result of what event?

> **A** Assassination **B** Impeachment **C** Coup d'Etat

9/11 ▶ Which of these actors has NOT won an Academy Award?

> **A** Cuba Gooding Jr **B** Louis Gossett Jr **C** Robert Downey Jr

9/12 ▶ Who reputedly said 'Everything should be made as simple as possible, but not any simpler'?

> **A** Albert Einstein **B** Steve Jobs **C** George W Bush

QUIZ 9

Head to Head – The Barrister Quiz 10

10/1 ▷ The name of the Spanish region Costa Brava roughly translates into English as what?

> **A** White Coast **B** Wild Coast **C** Windy Coast

10/2 ▷ Which Irish band won a Golden Globe for Best Song in 2014?

> **A** The Cranberries **B** The Script **C** U2

10/3 ▷ How does a creature known as a 'skipjack' move?

> **A** Fly **B** Run **C** Swim

10/4 ▷ Which of these posts has NOT been held by Kenneth Clarke?

> **A** Chancellor of the Exchequer **B** Home Secretary **C** Foreign Secretary

10/5 ▷ 'Umami', one of the five basic taste categories, detects what type of flavour?

> **A** Sweet **B** Savoury **C** Salty

10/6 ▷ Which of these conductors was the son of a famous 'pill millionaire'?

> **A** John Barbirolli **B** Thomas Beecham **C** Malcolm Sargent

10/7 ▷ Used to hunt animals, a 'tercel' is the male of what animal?

> **A** Hawk **B** Ferret **C** Bloodhound

10/8 ▷ The capital of which US state is named after army scout Kit Carson?

> **A** Colorado   **B** Nevada   **C** Arizona

10/9 ▷ Which of these dishes is NOT mentioned in the theme song of the TV comedy *Frasier*?

> **A** Tossed salads   **B** Mashed potato   **C** Scrambled eggs

10/10 ▷ Violinist Vanessa-Mae represented Thailand at the 2014 Winter Olympics in what event?

> **A** Giant slalom   **B** Figure skating   **C** Luge

10/11 ▷ Which rapper features on Katy Perry's Number One single 'California Gurls'?

> **A** 50 Cent   **B** Eminem   **C** Snoop Dogg

10/12 ▷ Which of these countries does NOT have the Queen as head of state?

> **A** Bahamas   **B** Bahrain   **C** Barbados

QUIZ 10

FINAL CHASE QUESTIONS

QUESTIONS

Final Chase Quiz 1

1/1 ▶ Complete the saying: 'Can't see the wood for the...' what?

1/2 ▶ The Scottish National Portrait Gallery is in what city?

1/3 ▶ What TV soap has a spin-off show called *Later*?

1/4 ▶ What's the English name for the Greek island of Kérkira?

1/5 ▶ What number follows 'Maroon' in the name of a chart-topping band?

1/6 ▶ Which horror writer also uses the pseudonym Richard Bachman?

1/7 ▶ Coco Rocha is a leading name in what fashion profession?

1/8 ▶ How many World Cups did Pelé win with Brazil?

1/9 ▶ What 2003 musical is set in the Land of Oz?

FINAL CHASE QUESTIONS

1/10 ▶ What transparent membrane covers the front of the eyeball?

1/11 ▶ The Beatrix Potter character Hunca Munca is what animal?

1/12 ▶ Zoë Saldana plays who in the film *Star Trek Into Darkness*?

1/13 ▶ The new Boeing 787 plane is also known by what one word?

1/14 ▶ Cheryl Cole has a tattoo of what flowers on her backside?

1/15 ▶ What Tchaikovsky ballet features the Arabian coffee dance?

1/16 ▶ The phrase 'vice versa' is from what language?

1/17 ▶ Tofu is usually what colour?

1/18 ▶ What country fought Britain at the Battle of Balaklava?

QUIZ 1

1/19 ▶ How many sequels of the film *Back to the Future* were made?

1/20 ▶ Spalding and Stamford are in what English county?

1/21 ▶ Cristoforo Colombo is the Italian name of which explorer?

1/22 ▶ What reality TV show is abbreviated C.B.B.?

1/23 ▶ Oprah Winfrey played Gloria Gaines in what 2013 film?

Final Chase Quiz 2

2/1 ▶ What first name links the poets Dryden and Keats?

2/2 ▶ What type of high street retailer is Wallis?

2/3 ▶ The planet Neptune orbits what star?

2/4 ▶ Mark Feehily was the youngest member of what Irish boy band?

FINAL CHASE QUESTIONS

2/5 ▶ Which explorer was knighted onboard ship at Deptford in 1581?

2/6 ▶ What musical is based on the book *Tevye and His Daughters*?

2/7 ▶ Tempering is a method for melting what confectionery?

2/8 ▶ Jack Donnelly plays Jason in what BBC fantasy drama?

2/9 ▶ Whose tea party was attended by the March Hare?

2/10 ▶ Pat Taaffe was a famous name in what sport?

2/11 ▶ Aberdeen Angus cattle are either 'Red' or what other colour?

2/12 ▶ 'I Turn to You' was a solo Number One for which Spice Girl?

2/13 ▶ What type of pastry is used to make a *religieuse*?

CHASE

2/14 ▶ What type of creature is a rudd?

2/15 ▶ Who played Stacey Slater in *EastEnders*?

2/16 ▶ A player starts a game of Scrabble with how many tiles?

2/17 ▶ Aalborg is a seaport in what European country?

2/18 ▶ *102 Dalmatians* is the sequel to what film?

2/19 ▶ What type of theatrical productions are *Giselle* and *Coppelia*?

2/20 ▶ Jonah Barrington was a famous name in what sport?

2/21 ▶ 'Shutter shades' are a type of what fashion accessory?

2/22 ▶ The towns of Eastleigh and Lymington are in what county?

2/23 ▶ What company made the iBook laptop computer?

Final Chase Quiz 3

3/1 ▶ Duke William of Normandy invaded England in what year?

3/2 ▶ Harrison Ford played Colonel Graff in what 2013 sci-fi film?

3/3 ▶ What children's book is the sequel to *The Gruffalo*?

3/4 ▶ Someone wanting to stand as an MP must be at least what age?

3/5 ▶ The Philippine Sea is part of what ocean?

3/6 ▶ The fibula runs parallel to what human bone?

3/7 ▶ Who served as senator for Illinois between 2005 and 2008?

3/8 ▶ Tatooine is a planet in what series of films?

3/9 ▶ Morty and Ferdie are nephews of which cartoon mouse?

3/10 ▶ The car company Mazda is based in what country?

3/11 ▶ George the Sixth became king in what decade?

3/12 ▶ America's big shopping day Black Friday is in what month?

3/13 ▶ What's the singular form of the word 'nuclei'?

3/14 ▶ Which brothers made the 2008 film *Burn After Reading*?

3/15 ▶ 'Tumble turns' are performed in what Olympic sport?

3/16 ▶ What letter did writer Arthur Quiller-Couch use as a pseudonym?

3/17 ▶ The RCAF is the Royal Air Force of what country?

3/18 ▶ Mars was the father of what mythological twins?

3/19 ▶ Mathew Horne plays headmaster Fraser in what sitcom?

3/20 ▶ What is the minimum number of darts required to score 501?

3/21 ▶ Headingley is a suburb of what Yorkshire city?

3/22 ▶ Which wartime Prime Minister owned a ginger cat called Jock?

3/23 ▶ What BBC legal drama is set in Shoe Lane Chambers?

Final Chase Quiz 4

4/1 ▶ What Shakespeare work is known as 'The Scottish Play'?

4/2 ▶ Trinidad and Tobago has coastlines on what ocean?

4/3 ▶ What species of mouse is Britain's smallest?

QUIZ 3–4

4/4 ▶ 'I heard it on my radio' is a line from what Queen song?

4/5 ▶ David Beckham played for what Italian club?

4/6 ▶ 'Elvish' is a fictional language created by which author?

4/7 ▶ *Lost and Found* was a book released by what dogs and cats home?

4/8 ▶ In yoga, the human body is said to contain how many chakras?

4/9 ▶ Which royal is Prince and Great Steward of Scotland?

4/10 ▶ What Rodgers and Hammerstein musical is set in Austria?

4/11 ▶ In the Old Testament, what book immediately follows Genesis?

4/12 ▶ What was the real first name of actor Rex Harrison?

FINAL CHASE QUESTIONS

4/13 ▶ Who played the title role in the 1959 film *Ben-Hur*?

4/14 ▶ A cravat is worn around what part of the body?

4/15 ▶ How many atoms of oxygen are in one molecule of water?

4/16 ▶ Which Dutch post-impressionist painted *The Night Café*?

4/17 ▶ *Kerplunk* and *Nimrod* are albums by what US band?

4/18 ▶ Which Wild West sharp-shooter was born Phoebe Ann Moses?

4/19 ▶ What nationality is the fictional detective Harry Hole?

4/20 ▶ Orion was a giant and hunter in what mythology?

4/21 ▶ What company developed the OS X computer operating system?

QUIZ 4

4/22 ▶ What voice type is singer Alfie Boe?

4/23 ▶ Stewie Griffin is a character in what animated TV series?

Final Chase Quiz 5

5/1 ▶ Which number Apollo mission did Alan Shepard command?

5/2 ▶ What breed of animal is a Hungarian puli?

5/3 ▶ Which writer created the character Captain Hook?

5/4 ▶ In the *Rocky Horror Show* where does Frank N Furter come from?

5/5 ▶ What is Sasha Obama's full first name?

5/6 ▶ The Hollywood Bowl is a concert venue in what US city?

5/7 ▶ What fish is used in the Scottish dish Tweed Kettle?

FINAL CHASE QUESTIONS

5/8 ▶ Which Democrat replaced Herbert Hoover as US President?

5/9 ▶ Which son of the singer Julio Iglesias was born in 1975?

5/10 ▶ The Vistula is which European country's longest river?

5/11 ▶ If you're bored and inactive, what are you said to twiddle?

5/12 ▶ What Lloyd Webber musical is based on poems by T S Eliot?

5/13 ▶ What's the third sign of the zodiac?

5/14 ▶ Who provided the vocals on Adamski's 1990 Number One 'Killer'?

5/15 ▶ In what country did Anne Frank write her diary?

5/16 ▶ What was the first space shuttle to orbit the Earth?

QUIZ 4–5

201

5/17 ▶ Press publicity can also be described as 'column...' what?

5/18 ▶ A Croat comes from what country?

5/19 ▶ Which gang in *West Side Story* shares its name with a fish?

5/20 ▶ During what war was the Gettysburg Address delivered?

5/21 ▶ Which author created the private investigator Cormoran Strike?

5/22 ▶ What Canadian city's name means 'Royal Mount' in French?

5/23 ▶ What imperial weight unit has the abbreviation 'c.w.t'?

Final Chase Quiz 6

6/1 ▶ Felpersham is a fictional place in what radio drama?

6/2 ▶ Fort Knox was named after which American Secretary of War?

FINAL CHASE QUESTIONS

6/3 ▶ Maidenhead and Marlow are towns on what river?

6/4 ▶ Aardvark is a navigator in what Joseph Heller novel?

6/5 ▶ What planet is named after a Roman god of agriculture?

6/6 ▶ Lana Lang was the teenage sweetheart of which superhero?

6/7 ▶ Newark Liberty Airport is in what American state?

6/8 ▶ What sport is played at the Middlesex Sevens tournament?

6/9 ▶ Grace Darling's father looked after what type of building?

6/10 ▶ The phrase 'ad lib' comes from what ancient language?

6/11 ▶ Which politician had the title Baroness of Kesteven?

6/12 ▶ Which female pop star had a 2014 hit with 'Dark Horse'?

6/13 ▶ Gascony is a historic region of what European country?

6/14 ▶ Literary character Anne Shirley lived on what farm?

6/15 ▶ 'Melon' is an anagram of what other fruit?

6/16 ▶ What number is written XC in Roman numerals?

6/17 ▶ Which sister of Castor and Pollux was abducted by Theseus?

6/18 ▶ Who wrote *The Lord of the Rings* books?

6/19 ▶ The island of Borneo is part of what continent?

6/20 ▶ What was banned in the US by the Eighteenth Amendment?

6/21 ▶ 'Gaz' Beadle found fame on what Newcastle-based reality TV show?

6/22 ▶ What party did Hillary Clinton represent in the US Senate?

6/23 ▶ What city is the county town of Essex?

Final Chase Quiz 7

7/1 ▶ A nun's wimple is usually what colour?

7/2 ▶ *Petals on the Wind* was a sequel to what V C Andrews book?

7/3 ▶ Who sold Harrods to Qatar Holding in 2010?

7/4 ▶ Marie-Antoinette's husband belonged to what royal dynasty?

7/5 ▶ Which architect designed the Guggenheim Museum in New York?

7/6 ▶ Whose is the third gospel in the New Testament?

7/7 ▶ How many stars on the state flag of Texas?

QUIZ 6–7

7/8 ▶ Prince Harry is officially 'Prince Henry of...' where?

7/9 ▶ *Mary Poppins, She Wrote* is a biography about which author?

7/10 ▶ How many grams in half a kilo?

7/11 ▶ Bundaberg rum comes from what country?

7/12 ▶ What animated TV show features the teacher Mr Garrison?

7/13 ▶ 'The Booth' is the 11th fence on what famous racecourse?

7/14 ▶ In what decade was Anthony Eden the British Prime Minister?

7/15 ▶ The Kremlin Armoury museum is in what city?

7/16 ▶ The song from musical *42nd Street* is 'Lullaby of...' where?

7/17 ▶ What space agency launched the Atlantis shuttle?

7/18 ▶ Who reached enlightenment in the village of Bodh Gaya in India?

7/19 ▶ The hat designer Philip Treacy was born in what country?

7/20 ▶ Which former House of Commons Speaker was called 'Gorbals Mick'?

7/21 ▶ A red star appears on the label of what famous Dutch beer?

7/22 ▶ *Aunts Aren't Gentlemen* was the last novel about which valet?

7/23 ▶ In what city did the philosopher Socrates die?

Final Chase Quiz 8

8/1 ▶ What stage musical features the drag queen Albin?

8/2 ▶ The word 'glockenspiel' comes from what language?

QUIZ 7–8

8/3 ▶ Which former Westlife member released the solo album *Home*?

8/4 ▶ What London art collection is in Manchester Square?

8/5 ▶ What Scottish city hosted the 1970 Commonwealth Games?

8/6 ▶ Which Apostle wrote the 'Epistle to the Philippians'?

8/7 ▶ How many 20th-century kings had the regnal name Edward?

8/8 ▶ Neil Diamond starred in the remake of what Al Jolson film?

8/9 ▶ The Pedro Miguel Locks are on what Central American canal?

8/10 ▶ What substance forms the hard glossy outer coating of teeth?

8/11 ▶ Balthamos and Baruch are angels in what Philip Pullman trilogy?

FINAL CHASE QUESTIONS

8/12 ▶ Stanley and Sheila Dwight were the parents of which singer?

8/13 ▶ Which Isle of Man cyclist was 2011 Road Race World Champion?

8/14 ▶ The symbol for danger is a skull and two crossed what?

8/15 ▶ 'Simoleon' is a fictional currency in what computer game series?

8/16 ▶ Lollo Rosso lettuce originated in what European country?

8/17 ▶ Which of the Queen's grandsons has no royal title?

8/18 ▶ Binky Felstead and Alex Mytton star in what reality show?

8/19 ▶ 'Testament of Youth' is a memoir by which female writer?

8/20 ▶ What is the world's largest Portuguese-speaking country?

8/21 ▶ Anthony Peter are the first names of which jockey?

8/22 ▶ The acronym CAL stands for 'Computer-Aided...' what?

8/23 ▶ Nicole Warren is a character in what F Scott Fitzgerald novel?

Final Chase Quiz 9

9/1 ▶ Jupiter was the supreme god in what mythology?

9/2 ▶ What is the name for a male badger?

9/3 ▶ Which poet wrote the line 'The proper study of Mankind is Man'?

9/4 ▶ Einstein completed his theory on what subject in 1915?

9/5 ▶ What is Wales' southernmost city?

FINAL CHASE QUESTIONS

9/6 ▶ 'If I Only Had a Brain' is a song from what classic film?

9/7 ▶ Who wrote the 1925 farce *Fallen Angels*?

9/8 ▶ The term 'blow-by-blow account' comes from what sport?

9/9 ▶ Aragon is a region of what European country?

9/10 ▶ Which king led England into the Hundred Years' War?

9/11 ▶ US film actor and director George Welles used what first name?

9/12 ▶ What nationality are the Papal guards at the Vatican?

9/13 ▶ What type of publications were *Buster* and *Beezer*?

9/14 ▶ The River Yare in Norfolk empties into what sea?

9/15 ▶ What was Queen Victoria's first language?

9/16 ▶ What motorway's southern end is in Devon?

9/17 ▶ Who wrote the screenplay for the 2013 film
Romeo & Juliet?

9/18 ▶ Which of the Fantastic Four has the real name
Susan Storm?

9/19 ▶ On a Monopoly board, what colour is Coventry
Street?

9/20 ▶ How many corners does a spinnaker sail have?

9/21 ▶ Elizabeth and Emmett were the neighbours in what
TV sitcom?

9/22 ▶ What's the first book in the Bible to begin with
a vowel?

9/23 ▶ What surname links chart-topping singers Dean
and Ricky?

Final Chase Quiz 10

10/1 ▷ Costa Teguise is on what Canary Island?

10/2 ▷ Ingrid was the daughter of what TV sitcom prisoner?

10/3 ▷ What Herman Melville novel has a chapter about 'Chowder'?

10/4 ▷ In America, the NYPD is the 'New York...' what?

10/5 ▷ *Geta* are worn on what part of the body by Japanese Geisha?

10/6 ▷ 'Backward pawn' and 'bad bishop' are terms in what game?

10/7 ▷ What flowers are named in the first line of 'My Favourite Things'?

10/8 ▷ Maribo is a cheese from what Nordic country?

10/9 ▷ What type of sporting venue is the Hippodrome de Longchamp?

10/10 ▶ What name links a Greek muse and a Renault car?

10/11 ▶ Bolognese sauce is named after a city in what country?

10/12 ▶ Theropods are a group of what extinct reptiles?

10/13 ▶ In 2014, who became host of *The Tonight Show* on US TV?

10/14 ▶ What's the only Portuguese-speaking country in South America?

10/15 ▶ Isaac Newton is buried in what London abbey?

10/16 ▶ In what decade did *Phantom of the Opera* open on Broadway?

10/17 ▶ Which author wrote the 2013 novel *Wedding Night*?

10/18 ▶ What Californian city's name comes from Saint Francis of Assisi?

10/19 ▶ Mola Ram is the villain in what Indiana Jones film?

FINAL CHASE QUESTIONS

10/20 ▶ In French, what simple piano tune is called *cutlets*?

10/21 ▶ Gian Domenico Cassini discovered four moons of what planet?

10/22 ▶ The WSOP is the World Series of what card game?

10/23 ▶ What sport was played by 'Shoeless' Joe Jackson?

Final Chase Quiz 11

11/1 ▶ What does the 'T' stand for in the trade union TSSA?

11/2 ▶ Who had a 1970s Number One album with *Sing It Again Rod*?

11/3 ▶ John Steinbeck won a Pulitzer Prize for what novel?

11/4 ▶ A zony is half pony and half what other animal?

11/5 ▶ Who wrote the classical piano trio called 'The Ghost'?

11/6 ▶ In newspaper announcements, 'obit' is short for what?

11/7 ▶ Frank Bruno lost to Mike Tyson twice in what Nevada city?

11/8 ▶ 'The Drugs Don't Work' was a Number One for what band?

11/9 ▶ Radar was developed before and during what war?

11/10 ▶ Cardinal Wolsey appears in what Shakespeare play?

11/11 ▶ The main forms of rugby in England are rugby union and what?

11/12 ▶ What dam is named after the 31st President of the US?

11/13 ▶ Which Nordic author wrote the *Oslo Sequence* of books?

FINAL CHASE QUESTIONS

11/14 ▶ Maggie Gyllenhaal played Elizabeth Darko in what film?

11/15 ▶ Which legendary knight was the adulterous lover of Guinevere?

11/16 ▶ Who came to the British throne in January 1936?

11/17 ▶ Which jockey retired in 1995 aged 59?

11/18 ▶ Which *Wizard of Oz* character has an Aunt called Em?

11/19 ▶ How many days after Hallowe'en is Bonfire Night?

11/20 ▶ What was the proper first name of Nell Gwyn?

11/21 ▶ The ancient city of Tanis is in what African country?

11/22 ▶ 'Pen and ink' is Cockney rhyming slang for what word?

11/23 ▶ What sport is played by the Delhi Daredevils?

Final Chase Quiz 12

12/1 ▶ What's the chemical symbol for the element Vanadium?

12/2 ▶ Which film director said: 'Blondes make the best victims'?

12/3 ▶ What folding chair is named after a platform on a ship?

12/4 ▶ What was the middle name of engineer Isambard Brunel?

12/5 ▶ Which actor was both a Blues Brother and a Ghostbuster?

12/6 ▶ Red Robbo is the nickname of which 1970s trade unionist?

12/7 ▶ What novel has a chapter called 'Fagin's Last Night Alive'?

12/8 ▶ The name of what Monaco resort means 'Mount Charles'?

FINAL CHASE QUESTIONS

12/9 ▶ In what decade did Damien Hirst win the Turner Prize?

12/10 ▶ In 1966, which astronaut commanded *Gemini 8*?

12/11 ▶ 'Hello possums' is the catchphrase of which comedy character?

12/12 ▶ Which singer came second to Diversity on *Britain's Got Talent*?

12/13 ▶ The A350 aircraft is made by what European plane company?

12/14 ▶ Who was the youngest daughter of Tsar Nicholas the Second?

12/15 ▶ In beer-making, East Kent Goldings is what type of plant?

12/16 ▶ In Christianity, the Trinity is the Father, Son and what else?

12/17 ▶ The Sony games console PSP stands for 'Playstation...' what?

QUIZ 12

12/18 ▶ Les Kellett was a famous name in what sport?

12/19 ▶ In the nursery rhyme, whose name rhymes with 'see-saw'?

12/20 ▶ The digestive tract is also known as the 'alimentary...' what?

12/21 ▶ What's the most populated city in France?

12/22 ▶ In what TV show did Paula Yates interview guests on a bed?

12/23 ▶ John Vorster was Prime Minister and President of what country?

Final Chase Quiz 13

13/1 ▶ 'Guilty' is a fragrance by what Italian fashion house?

13/2 ▶ Bottles of Malibu liqueur are normally what colour?

13/3 ▶ In what decade did the first Hard Rock Café open?

FINAL CHASE QUESTIONS

13/4 ▶ Which American TV mobster was the only son of Livia?

13/5 ▶ On what part of the body did Ancient Greeks wear a petasus?

13/6 ▶ How many Xs are there on the Castlemaine beer logo?

13/7 ▶ In Cockney rhyming slang, what is 'bread and honey'?

13/8 ▶ In 1899, Lord Curzon was appointed Viceroy of where?

13/9 ▶ What Japanese company released the 'Saturn' games console?

13/10 ▶ The phrase 'In at the deep end' comes from what leisure activity?

13/11 ▶ An auriscope is used to examine what part of the body?

13/12 ▶ What relation is actress Bridget Fonda to Jane Fonda?

13/13 ▶ Graham Greene's *The Honorary Consul* is set in what country?

13/14 ▶ 'Fizz' is a nickname for what French sparkling wine?

13/15 ▶ The Mall links Buckingham Palace to what square?

13/16 ▶ Who directed and starred in the film *Easy Rider*?

13/17 ▶ The 'Man in the Iron Mask' was a prisoner of which French king?

13/18 ▶ What animal is a Swedish elkhound?

13/19 ▶ The Lindy Hop was introduced to Britain during what war?

13/20 ▶ What shape does Teletubby Tinky Winky have on his head?

13/21 ▶ Fiyero is a character in what musical?

13/22 ▶ The Caledonian Canal links the North Sea with what ocean?

13/23 ▶ How was darts player John Thomas Wilson better known?

Final Chase Quiz 14

14/1 ▶ What did Einstein call the 'Fourth Dimension'?

14/2 ▶ The Kuban River is in what country?

14/3 ▶ Scarlet Gala is a variety of what fruit?

14/4 ▶ What first name is shared by poets Marvell and Motion?

14/5 ▶ 'Steamy Windows' was a 1990 hit for which US singer?

14/6 ▶ What Asian capital is known to its locals as 'Krung Thep'?

14/7 ▶ Which male superhero came to Earth from Krypton?

14/8 ▶ What drink is celebrated at Munich's Oktoberfest?

14/9 ▶ What's the last volume in *The Lord of the Rings* trilogy?

14/10 ▶ 'A Little Time' was a Number One hit in 1990 for what band?

14/11 ▶ The sarong originated on what continent?

14/12 ▶ Pride Rock is a setting in what Disney film?

14/13 ▶ What's nine multiplied by six?

14/14 ▶ Liam Howlett was the founder member of what dance music group?

14/15 ▶ American Michael Johnson commentates on what sport on TV?

14/16 ▶ 'Treasure' was a 2013 hit for which American pop star?

14/17 ▶ What is the largest moon to orbit Neptune?

FINAL CHASE QUESTIONS

14/18 ▶ What first name was shared by two of the Spice Girls?

14/19 ▶ What video game franchise is abbreviated to COD?

14/20 ▶ Snuff comes from the leaves of which plant?

14/21 ▶ Which chef released the *Proper Pub Food* cookbook?

14/22 ▶ What first name links actors Astin, Bean and Connery?

14/23 ▶ Which manager signed Wayne Rooney for Manchester United?

Final Chase Quiz 15

15/1 ▶ What does a nucivorous animal feed on?

15/2 ▶ Who did Carla Bruni marry in 2008?

15/3 ▶ 'Beautiful Life' was a 2013 hit for what *X Factor* boy band?

15/4 ▶ 'Jack the Ripper' is cockney rhyming slang for what cured fish?

15/5 ▶ In the famous opera, in what city was Figaro a barber?

15/6 ▶ *The Guts* by Roddy Doyle is a sequel to what 1987 novel?

15/7 ▶ On what cartoon would you hear the phrase 'Yabba-Dabba-Doo'?

15/8 ▶ The Esquiline is one of what city's seven hills?

15/9 ▶ In what country was singer Daniel Bedingfield born?

15/10 ▶ How many 'varieties' are there in the Heinz slogan?

15/11 ▶ Macavity is a character in what Andrew Lloyd Webber musical?

FINAL CHASE QUESTIONS

15/12 ▶ 'Sexy Chick' was a 2009 Number One hit for which Frenchman?

15/13 ▶ What's nine times eight?

15/14 ▶ 'Miu Miu' is a fashion brand named after which designer?

15/15 ▶ Ladybirds are from what order of insects?

15/16 ▶ Who plays the 'The Great Gatsby' in the 2013 film?

15/17 ▶ Chelsea footballer Eden Hazard plays for what country?

15/18 ▶ Which politician led Cuba for 49 years?

15/19 ▶ What zodiac constellation lies between Aries and Gemini?

15/20 ▶ What's the full name of the document known as a CV?

QUIZ 15

15/21 ▶ The composer Johann Sebastian Bach was born in what century?

15/22 ▶ Which Shakespeare title character becomes king of Scotland?

15/23 ▶ Chalkhill blue is a species of what insect?

Final Chase Quiz 16

16/1 ▶ Charlotte Crosby found fame on what MTV reality show?

16/2 ▶ Who wrote *The Tale of Johnny Town-Mouse*?

16/3 ▶ 'Start of Something New' is a song from what Disney teen film?

16/4 ▶ Junius was the Latin name for what month?

16/5 ▶ What number puzzles were invented by Howard Garns in 1979?

16/6 ▶ Which queen of France was the 11th daughter of Maria Theresa?

16/7 ▶ Traditionally, what primary colour indicates a hot water tap?

16/8 ▶ In what city would you see a Hammers-Eagles football derby?

16/9 ▶ Futomaki are thick rolls of what Japanese food?

16/10 ▶ Harrison Ford was Oscar-nominated for what 1980s film?

16/11 ▶ In 1975, which nurse first appeared on the £10 note?

16/12 ▶ Nereus was a sea god in what ancient mythology?

16/13 ▶ What house did Elvis Presley move into in 1957?

16/14 ▶ Which American crime writer created the detective Mike Hammer?

16/15 ▶ In what decade did people last walk on the moon?

QUIZ 15–16

16/16 ▶ Which girl band released the Sport Relief single 'Word Up!'?

16/17 ▶ David Davies won silver at the Beijing Olympics in what sport?

16/18 ▶ What's half of 54?

16/19 ▶ The Metrocentre shopping complex is in what north-east town?

16/20 ▶ Which son of Adam and Eve killed his brother?

16/21 ▶ Which actor is best known for playing Freddy Krueger?

16/22 ▶ What type of weapon was King Arthur's Excalibur?

16/23 ▶ Retinitis pigmentosa affects what sensory organ?

Final Chase Quiz 17

17/1 ▶ What fashion house makes the 'Fuel for Life' fragrance?

FINAL CHASE QUESTIONS

17/2 ▶ In the saying, what shouldn't you look 'in the mouth'?

17/3 ▶ Which boy band had the world's best-selling album of 2013?

17/4 ▶ What first name links Russian leaders Lenin and Putin?

17/5 ▶ In the zodiac, what month does Cancer turn into Leo?

17/6 ▶ What Welsh new town has a name meaning 'Valley of the Raven'?

17/7 ▶ What preserve is part of a traditional cream tea?

17/8 ▶ At the Sydney Olympics, what sport was held on Bondi Beach?

17/9 ▶ Weston-super-Mare is a resort in what county?

17/10 ▶ What film was the sequel to 'The Bourne Ultimatum'?

17/11 ▶ What's 20 percent of 500?

17/12 ▶ In legend, whose ninth labour was to fetch Hippolyta's girdle?

17/13 ▶ Redruth is a market town in what county?

17/14 ▶ 'V' is a perfume by which Italian fashion house?

17/15 ▶ Dermatophobia is the fear of disease in what part of the body?

17/16 ▶ 'Unbreakable' was a Number One hit for what Irish boy band?

17/17 ▶ By what name was Hull-born poet Florence Margaret Smith known?

17/18 ▶ The battle of Culloden took place in what country of the UK?

17/19 ▶ Which actor won his third Oscar for the film *Lincoln*?

17/20 ▶ On what continent is the River Tigris?

17/21 ▶ What French dance music duo released the album 'Discovery'?

17/22 ▶ 'Blood' and 'Seville' are types of what citrus fruit?

17/23 ▶ A cochlear implant is placed in what sensory organ?

Final Chase Quiz 18

18/1 ▶ What ballet centres on a young man falling in love with a doll?

18/2 ▶ Devon Malcolm represented England at what sport?

18/3 ▶ Egypt's highest state honour is named after what river?

18/4 ▶ How many adenoids are found at the back of the nose?

18/5 ▶ Who did director Ron Howard play in TV's *Happy Days*?

QUIZ 17–18

18/6 ▶ Which of the Channel Islands is closest to mainland Britain?

18/7 ▶ 'Air' and 'Thirteen' are rides at what UK theme park?

18/8 ▶ What is the second book of the Bible called?

18/9 ▶ What famous Australian bridge opened in 1932?

18/10 ▶ What nationality is the model Lara Stone?

18/11 ▶ Who's the film star brother of actress Joan Cusack?

18/12 ▶ What's the shorter of the two bones of the forearm?

18/13 ▶ Iris, Ceres and Juno are spirits in what Shakespeare play?

18/14 ▶ In the Royal Navy, the letters CPO represent what rank?

18/15 ▶ Terry Waite was kidnapped in what Middle Eastern country?

FINAL CHASE QUESTIONS

18/16 ▶ Scott's Hut is an explorer's cabin on what continent?

18/17 ▶ The 2014 film *Need for Speed* stars which *Breaking Bad* actor?

18/18 ▶ A Belisha beacon is mounted on a post of what two colours?

18/19 ▶ Queen Victoria's husband Albert was born in what modern-day country?

18/20 ▶ Which British architect designed the Millennium Dome?

18/21 ▶ Barbara and Margo were main characters in what classic sitcom?

18/22 ▶ What month is named after the Roman god of war?

18/23 ▶ What number links the Deadly Sins and Disney's dwarfs?

Final Chase Quiz 19

19/1 ▶ Who became de facto leader of Libya in 1969?

19/2 ▶ What Sheffield band won five prizes at the 2014 NME awards?

19/3 ▶ Lord Skrumshus is a character in what Ian Fleming novel?

19/4 ▶ The expression 'sucker punch' comes from what sport?

19/5 ▶ Played by Paul Whitehouse, Rowley Birkin QC was a character in what TV show?

19/6 ▶ Operation Dragoon was an invasion of France in what war?

19/7 ▶ In 1815, Annabella Milbanke married which poet?

19/8 ▶ What European language is an official language of Peru?

19/9 ▶ The East Village is part of what New York borough?

19/10 ▶ 'Russians' was a solo hit for what member of the Police?

19/11 ▶ In the human body, T-cells are named after what gland?

19/12 ▶ In *The Simpsons*, what is Bart's name short for?

19/13 ▶ What gossip magazine runs an annual 'Weird Crush' poll?

19/14 ▶ Who was in charge of the inquiry into the Profumo Affair?

19/15 ▶ What bingo number is nicknamed 'clickety click'?

19/16 ▶ Which female pop star released the 2014 song 'Air Balloon'?

19/17 ▶ North Ronaldsay is a breed of what farm animal?

19/18 ▶ QMG is an abbreviation for what army position?

19/19 ▶ The adjective 'Venusian' refers to what planet?

19/20 ▶ What large wetland area is in southern Florida?

19/21 ▶ What Verdi opera is about a princess of Ethiopia?

19/22 ▶ Each suit in a pack of cards has how many court cards?

19/23 ▶ Who was best man at Joseph Goebbels' wedding?

Final Chase Quiz 20

20/1 ▶ Buck House is a nickname for what royal residence?

20/2 ▶ Fish eggs are known by what three-letter name?

20/3 ▶ Ermine Street was a famous road built by what empire?

20/4 ▶ Thomson's gazelle is native to what continent?

FINAL CHASE QUESTIONS

20/5 ▶ Suranne Jones played Sister Joan Livesey in what TV drama?

20/6 ▶ What Cornish fishing village is at the mouth of the river Pol?

20/7 ▶ Jiangsu is a province of what country?

20/8 ▶ What does the agency Elite World specialise in?

20/9 ▶ Traditionally how many columns are there on a sudoku grid?

20/10 ▶ The volcano Elysium Mons is on what planet?

20/11 ▶ Lake Como is the deepest lake in what European country?

20/12 ▶ Illustrator Aubrey Beardsley lived in what century?

20/13 ▶ The prehistoric site Woodhenge is in what county?

20/14 ▶ Wanda Gershwitz is a character in what 1980s film comedy?

20/15 ▶ Cantabria is a region of what European country?

20/16 ▶ Panther Cap is a poisonous type of what?

20/17 ▶ The Magritte awards are film prizes in what country?

20/18 ▶ Which football manager wrote the book *Sven: My Story*?

20/19 ▶ Receptors in the eye react to what stimulus?

20/20 ▶ Which stand-up comedian hosts his *Comedy Vehicle* TV show?

20/21 ▶ The Royal Northern College of Music is based in what city?

20/22 ▶ What breed of dog is the Irish Guards' mascot?

20/23 ▶ What nationality is chef Raymond Blanc?

Final Chase Quiz 21

21/1 ▶ Who presented the ITV show *Trisha*?

21/2 ▶ How many counties formed the historic Irish province of Ulster?

21/3 ▶ Who played the title role in the boxing film *Ali*?

21/4 ▶ *Muchas gracias* is 'many thanks' in what language?

21/5 ▶ What's the largest city by population in Germany?

21/6 ▶ Which member of The Who wrote the song 'My Generation'?

21/7 ▶ What species of sturgeon is also known as the 'hausen'?

21/8 ▶ Sparta was a city-state in what European country?

QUIZ 20–21

21/9 ▶ Dr Izzie Stevens was a character in what TV hospital drama?

21/10 ▶ Mahatma Gandhi was born in what century?

21/11 ▶ Which Hungarian composer introduced Chopin to George Sand?

21/12 ▶ Cross stitch is a style of what decorative needlework?

21/13 ▶ Which king defeated the Persians at the Battle of Issus?

21/14 ▶ What appointment did Thomas Gray decline in 1757?

21/15 ▶ What type of salad ingredient is a pomodorino?

21/16 ▶ Paterson Joseph plays Johnson in what Mitchell and Webb sitcom?

21/17 ▶ Which Icelandic broadcaster wrote the book *The Vikings*?

21/18 ▶ What is the UK's longest-running radio show?

21/19 ▶ What colour is the packaging on chicken OXO cubes?

21/20 ▶ The resort of Cancún is located on what sea?

21/21 ▶ *Home* was a Number One album for what drum and bass group?

21/22 ▶ Most of the asteroids in our solar system orbit what body?

21/23 ▶ In the body a 'venule' is a small or minor what?

Final Chase Quiz 22

22/1 ▶ In what city does Oliver Twist join a gang of pickpockets?

22/2 ▶ What lengthy war began in 1337?

22/3 ▶ What was the sequel to the Rowan Atkinson film *Bean*?

22/4 ▶ Beale Street is a famous road in what Tennessee city?

22/5 ▶ What creature is a lilac-breasted roller?

22/6 ▶ The National Centre for what sport is in Roehampton?

22/7 ▶ Braemar is in what national park?

22/8 ▶ Albuquerque in New Mexico stands on what river?

22/9 ▶ Which scientist wrote the book *The Double Helix*?

22/10 ▶ What ballet company's name means 'Big' in Russian?

22/11 ▶ Alf Stewart is the longest-surviving character in what TV soap?

22/12 ▶ What raw seafood delicacy is often served 'on the half shell'?

FINAL CHASE QUESTIONS

22/13 ▶ In the TESSA saving scheme, what did the 'A' stand for?

22/14 ▶ What fruit is known in Spanish as a *plátano*?

22/15 ▶ Noddy wears what colour top?

22/16 ▶ Boscastle is a village on the northern coast of what county?

22/17 ▶ 'Memory' was the only Top Ten solo hit for what musical star?

22/18 ▶ Great Orme in Wales was noted for the mining of what metal?

22/19 ▶ Flim-flam is an old name for what Olympic sport?

22/20 ▶ What musical term comes from the Italian word for 'time'?

22/21 ▶ What small fish are used to make tapenade?

22/22 ▶ What bone in birds is two collar-bones fused together?

22/23 ▶ Richmond is the capital of what American state?

Final Chase Quiz 23

23/1 ▶ The musical *Cabaret* is set in what country?

23/2 ▶ What character did Henry Thomas play in the film *ET*?

23/3 ▶ Sapphire is the traditional birthstone of what month?

23/4 ▶ The Gazelle River is on what continent?

23/5 ▶ In what century was the Great Vine planted at Hampton Court?

23/6 ▶ 'Bangs' is the American term for what hair feature?

23/7 ▶ 'Wherever I Lay My Hat' was a Number One for which singer?

FINAL CHASE QUESTIONS

23/8 ▶ Nottingham's ice hockey team is named after what big cats?

23/9 ▶ The Blarney Stone is made of what rock?

23/10 ▶ What nationality is 'Chariots of Fire' composer Vangelis?

23/11 ▶ Valpolicella is an Italian variety of what drink?

23/12 ▶ *Any Answers* is a programme on what BBC radio station?

23/13 ▶ The Telemark Canal is in what Scandinavian country?

23/14 ▶ Victor is the first name of what Mary Shelley title character?

23/15 ▶ Who was the Beatles' lead guitarist?

23/16 ▶ The manned space satellite in *Thunderbirds* has what number?

23/17 ▶ What alpine flower features in a *Sound of Music* song?

23/18 ▶ Golf's US Masters is played in what month?

23/19 ▶ What language is spoken in a Hispanophone country?

23/20 ▶ Which French author wrote *Five Weeks in a Balloon*?

23/21 ▶ In Disney's *Aladdin*, what creature is Abu?

23/22 ▶ *Bluff* magazine is devoted to what card game?

23/23 ▶ In the regulation of British tennis, what does LTA stand for?

Final Chase Quiz 24

24/1 ▶ The Indian city of Patna is on what sacred river?

24/2 ▶ *All the Lost Souls* was a hit album for which singer?

FINAL CHASE QUESTIONS

24/3 ▶ What form of theatrical dance features 'pointe work'?

24/4 ▶ What term for a disorderly crowd is a nickname for the Mafia?

24/5 ▶ What art movement was founded by Hugo Ball in World War One?

24/6 ▶ What country annexed the Orkney Islands in 1472?

24/7 ▶ Michael Caine played soldier Gonville Bromhead in what film?

24/8 ▶ The Russian drink 'Yorsh' is beer mixed with what spirit?

24/9 ▶ Who succeeded Gray Davis as Governor of California in 2003?

24/10 ▶ How many fluid ounces in half a pint?

24/11 ▶ The Rusholme 'curry mile' is an area in what city?

24/12 ▶ Singer Val Doonican came from what country?

24/13 ▶ The ski resort of Aspen is in what mountain range?

24/14 ▶ The Bald Eagle has what colour feathers on its head?

24/15 ▶ The name of what leg bone is from the Latin for 'brooch'?

24/16 ▶ Lithuania's coastline is on what sea?

24/17 ▶ Laurel and Hardy wore what type of hat?

24/18 ▶ Who began a second US presidential term in 2013?

24/19 ▶ 'You may say I'm a dreamer' is a lyric from what John Lennon song?

24/20 ▶ Peter Phillips's wife Autumn was born in what country?

24/21 ▶ In cooking, what's the common name for potassium bitartrate?

24/22 ▶ What women's athletics event takes place over two days?

24/23 ▶ Nat 'King' Cole began his career as a player of what instrument?

Final Chase Quiz 25

25/1 ▶ Bradycardia is the slowing of what body organ?

25/2 ▶ Who presents the ITV show *Big Star's Little Star*?

25/3 ▶ Shakespeare's play is *The Two Gentlemen of...* where?

25/4 ▶ What's the only US state named after a President?

25/5 ▶ What British sports car brand makes the XK Coupé?

25/6 ▶ Granville and Gladys were characters in what TV sitcom?

25/7 ▶ The name of what foodstuff is the Italian word for dough?

25/8 ▶ Canadian province Nova Scotia is in what ocean?

25/9 ▶ Which singer featured on the Lady Gaga song 'Do What U Want'?

25/10 ▶ What is four-fifths of 100?

25/11 ▶ What's the stage name of comedian Lee Gordon McKillop?

25/12 ▶ 'Very Irresistible' is a perfume by what French fashion house?

25/13 ▶ What rhyming phrase for an upset stomach includes a city in India?

25/14 ▶ What Roddy Doyle novel became a West End musical in 2013?

25/15 ▶ What 'hole' can be formed by the collapse of a massive star?

25/16 ▶ 'Final Score' was originally part of what TV sports programme?

25/17 ▶ What Tchaikovsky ballet is based on an E T A Hoffmann story?

25/18 ▶ In Norse legend, the Valkyries were sent into battle by whom?

25/19 ▶ 'Currant bun' is cockney rhyming slang for what heavenly body?

25/20 ▶ What athletics event is just over 42 kilometres long?

25/21 ▶ What French fashion house makes the fragrance 'Égoïste'?

25/22 ▶ Which rock band called their 2013 album *Rewind the Film*?

25/23 ▶ Exmoor horn is a breed of what animal?

Final Chase Quiz 26

26/1 ▶ What Botticelli painting is also called *Venus on the Half Shell*?

26/2 ▶ A Castilian comes from a region in what country?

26/3 ▶ The song 'A Star is Born' features in what Disney cartoon film?

26/4 ▶ The Yellow Hat sect is a Tibetan order in what religion?

26/5 ▶ Mrs Bird is the housekeeper at the home of which bear?

26/6 ▶ Who married Thomas Seymour after Henry the Eighth died?

26/7 ▶ *The Showgirl Princess* was a book by which Australian singer?

26/8 ▶ The Republic of the Marshall Islands is in what ocean?

26/9 ▶ Rats belong to what order of mammals?

26/10 ▶ Who was the first US President to have a hotline with Moscow?

FINAL CHASE QUESTIONS

26/11 ▶ What's two thirds of 45?

26/12 ▶ M10 9KC is the postcode for a road in what TV soap?

26/13 ▶ Which Football League team is nicknamed The Cumbrians?

26/14 ▶ 'Dim sum' is a style of eating in what cuisine?

26/15 ▶ What Italian fashion house created the perfume 'Rush'?

26/16 ▶ 'Steed' is a poetic name for what animal?

26/17 ▶ Bill and Ben Porter were the parents in what sitcom?

26/18 ▶ The song 'As If We Never Said Goodbye' is from what musical?

26/19 ▶ The two Voyager spacecraft were launched from what cape?

26/20 ▶ What Scottish city is served by Turnhouse Airport?

26/21 ▶ In 2013, who had a hit with 'Bonfire Heart'?

26/22 ▶ In *Gone With The Wind*, which character had three husbands?

26/23 ▶ Which biblical king had sons called Daniel and Absalom?

Final Chase Quiz 27

27/1 ▶ What ocean shares its name with an Asian nationality?

27/2 ▶ How many farthings made up a pre-decimal penny?

27/3 ▶ On TV, who presents *Relocation, Relocation* with Phil Spencer?

27/4 ▶ The Battle of Gettysburg took place in what century?

27/5 ▶ Nick Barmby played what sport for England?

FINAL CHASE QUESTIONS

27/6 ▶ Ogden Nash wrote 'Candy is Dandy but Liquor is...' what?

27/7 ▶ Queen's gambit is an opening set of moves in what board game?

27/8 ▶ Cruorin is a former name for what blood pigment?

27/9 ▶ The 1970s TV show *Kojak* was set in what American city?

27/10 ▶ Who became Poet Laureate in 2009?

27/11 ▶ 'Speleology' is the study of what natural feature?

27/12 ▶ In Disney's *Cinderella*, who are Drizella and Anastasia?

27/13 ▶ What items are kept in the British Museum's Duveen Gallery?

27/14 ▶ What's the brightest heavenly body as seen from Earth?

27/15 ▶ Who was King of England 100 years ago?

27/16 ▶ Which US performer released the album *My Name is Barbra*?

27/17 ▶ What ingredient is at the centre of a Baked Alaska?

27/18 ▶ After his final battle, King Arthur was taken to what island?

27/19 ▶ What film had the tagline 'They ain't afraid of no ghost'?

27/20 ▶ Albuquerque is the largest city in what American state?

27/21 ▶ What name is given to the holiday taken by newlyweds?

27/22 ▶ The adjective 'tigrine' refers to what animal?

27/23 ▶ Which pianist composed 'Fig Leaf Rag' and 'Magnetic Rag'?

Final Chase Quiz 28

28/1 ▶ Don Brown's book *One Giant Leap* is about which astronaut?

28/2 ▶ Taleggio cheese comes from what country?

28/3 ▶ Aaron Johnson played which Beatle in the film *Nowhere Boy*?

28/4 ▶ Brahmanism developed into what major religion?

28/5 ▶ How many people are there in a synchronised diving team?

28/6 ▶ What's the largest city on the island of Honshu?

28/7 ▶ Which beer brand claimed it was 'the Australian for lager'?

28/8 ▶ Mr Worldly Wiseman appears in what John Bunyan work?

28/9 ▶ In Greek myth, what flying horse was ridden by Bellerophon?

28/10 ▶ Who won his second acting Oscar for the film *Milk*?

28/11 ▶ What city in Burma is also known as Rangoon?

28/12 ▶ 'Window In The Skies' was a hit for which Irish rock band?

28/13 ▶ Spain and what other country joined the EEC in 1986?

28/14 ▶ What weight is one-fourteenth of a stone?

28/15 ▶ Which royal is patron of the Scottish Rugby Union?

28/16 ▶ What fruit gives guacamole its green colour?

28/17 ▶ What first name links authors Hardy, Hughes and Harris?

28/18 ▶ The Peasants Revolt took place in what century?

28/19 ▶ What long-running TV quiz has a QS logo?

FINAL CHASE QUESTIONS

28/20 ▶ The gnu is an animal native to what continent?

28/21 ▶ How is singer Robert Peter Williams more commonly known?

28/22 ▶ The throne of which supreme Greek god was at Mount Olympus?

28/23 ▶ What Ukrainian football team won 13 Soviet league titles?

Final Chase Quiz 29

29/1 ▶ Playhouse is another name for what entertainment venue?

29/2 ▶ WCW was a championship in what sports entertainment?

29/3 ▶ What is Rocky Balboa's proper first name?

29/4 ▶ The aviator Charles Kingsford Smith was born in what country?

29/5 ▶ 'Hazel's Decision' is a chapter in what Richard Adams' novel?

29/6 ▶ Freddie Trumper is an American Grand Master in what musical?

29/7 ▶ Two members of what band starred in the film *The Krays*?

29/8 ▶ Who manned the final NASA Gemini flight with James Lovell?

29/9 ▶ Braga is a city in what European country?

29/10 ▶ Which Scandinavian dramatist wrote *The Pillars of Society*?

29/11 ▶ Which glam rocker changed his stage name from Shane Fenton?

29/12 ▶ In what decade did England's Premier Football League begin?

29/13 ▶ What London cathedral was designed by John Francis Bentley?

FINAL CHASE QUESTIONS

29/14 ▶ The Red Road flats complex was built in what Scottish city?

29/15 ▶ What Commonwealth capital began as Port Nicholson in 1840?

29/16 ▶ The Irish bread known as fadge is made with what vegetables?

29/17 ▶ Rodeo Drive is a famous shopping street in what American state?

29/18 ▶ In the novel, which commanding officer causes *The Caine Mutiny*?

29/19 ▶ The hormone oestrogen is primarily produced in what organs?

29/20 ▶ 'Stars Are Blind' was a hit single for which socialite?

29/21 ▶ According to the saying, 'seek and ye shall...' what?

29/22 ▶ Since 2007, Ban Ki-Moon has held what UN office?

29/23 ▶ Polycotton is a fabric combining cotton and what material?

Final Chase Quiz 30

30/1 ▶ What was 'Tainted' in the title of a Soft Cell Number One?

30/2 ▶ What Nobel Laureate was the daughter of an Albanian grocer?

30/3 ▶ Alexander Pope wrote 'Hope springs eternal in the human...' what?

30/4 ▶ On what continent does Demerara sugar originate?

30/5 ▶ Which ruler was married to Empress Nagako of Japan?

30/6 ▶ What 1989 film featured a chauffeur called Hoke?

30/7 ▶ Which Italian fashion house makes the 'Sicily' range of bags?

30/8 ▶ What Scottish city stands on the River Ness?

FINAL CHASE QUESTIONS

30/9 ▶ What type of creature is a 'silver biddy'?

30/10 ▶ 'Lightning Returns' is an instalment in what video game series?

30/11 ▶ Jerry Hall was born in what American state?

30/12 ▶ Anthony Powell's major work is *A Dance to the Music of...* what?

30/13 ▶ Heinrich Himmler belonged to what political party?

30/14 ▶ What's the southernmost country on the Balkan Peninsula?

30/15 ▶ *The Armstrong Lie* is a documentary about which cyclist?

30/16 ▶ Enrico is the Italian equivalent of what English boy's name?

30/17 ▶ What does the royal title HBM stand for?

30/18 ▶ 'The Flying Dutchman' was a class in what Olympic sport?

30/19 ▶ What bird species are Skipper and Rico in the *Madagascar* films?

30/20 ▶ What colour are the olive branches on the flag of Cyprus?

30/21 ▶ What Finnish company created the N series of smartphones?

30/22 ▶ In what century did Edvard Munch first paint *The Scream*?

30/23 ▶ 'Weegie' is a slang term for someone from what Scottish city?

Final Chase Quiz 31

31/1 ▶ 'Legend of the Lamp' is a song in what Disney film?

31/2 ▶ Which captain gave Botany Bay in Australia its name?

FINAL CHASE QUESTIONS

31/3 ▶ Pianist Victor Borge was born in what European country?

31/4 ▶ What is the chemical symbol for nitrogen?

31/5 ▶ Which American was the original presenter of *Masterchef*?

31/6 ▶ In the well-known saying, what follows 'Penny wise'?

31/7 ▶ The name of what constellation means 'Greater Dog' in Latin?

31/8 ▶ What country does footballer Lionel Messi come from?

31/9 ▶ Singer Lyle Lovett was the first husband of which Hollywood star?

31/10 ▶ Who wrote *The Forsyte Saga* series of novels?

31/11 ▶ 'CK Be' is a fragrance by which fashion house?

31/12 ▶ Statics is a branch of which of the three main sciences?

31/13 ▶ The American city of San Diego lies on what ocean?

31/14 ▶ Which Irish actress joined the cast of *EastEnders* in 2014?

31/15 ▶ What's three quarters of 200?

31/16 ▶ Which German composer began going deaf in 1801?

31/17 ▶ Famed for her hats, who was nicknamed 'The Ascot mascot'?

31/18 ▶ *Only the Lonely* is a musical about which American singer?

31/19 ▶ Detective Fix is a policeman in what Jules Verne novel?

31/20 ▶ What cartoon was originally called 'The Flagstones'?

31/21 ▶ *Giallo* is the Italian word for what primary colour?

31/22 ▶ If it's summer in the UK, what season is it in Australia?

31/23 ▶ The song 'Greased Lightning' is about what type of vehicle?

Final Chase Quiz 32

32/1 ▶ Which king was the present Queen's grandfather?

32/2 ▶ In Tennyson's poem, what cavalry division are 'the six hundred'?

32/3 ▶ What island forms a Commonwealth country with Nevis?

32/4 ▶ Which James Bond actor was born in Drogheda, Ireland?

32/5 ▶ Bel Paese cheese gets its name from what language?

32/6 ▶ What German dog was formerly called the wire-haired pinscher?

32/7 ▶ The American War of Independence took place in what century?

32/8 ▶ D I Jardine was the sidekick of which Scottish TV detective?

32/9 ▶ Herod and Herodias are characters in what Oscar Wilde play?

32/10 ▶ What football club sacked David Moyes in April 2014?

32/11 ▶ The Goya Gate is an entrance at what Madrid museum?

32/12 ▶ How many clavicle bones are in the human body?

32/13 ▶ In 2010, which female singer had a Number One with 'Once'?

32/14 ▶ What's half of one-sixth?

32/15 ▶ The Taj Mahal is mainly built from what colour marble?

32/16 ▶ What relation is the Princess Royal to Prince Harry?

32/17 ▶ Fans of which American singer are known as 'Grobanites'?

32/18 ▶ What city comes between Kilo and Mike in the NATO alphabet?

32/19 ▶ Which Dr Who assistant was played by Elisabeth Sladen?

32/20 ▶ The 1982 FIFA World Cup was hosted by what country?

32/21 ▶ What animated film series features Marty the Zebra?

32/22 ▶ The Marshall Plan was implemented under what US President?

32/23 ▶ Battenburg cake is covered with a paste of what nut?

Final Chase Quiz 33

33/1 ▶ What 1970s soul-funk group were sometimes known as 'EWF'?

33/2 ▶ Haneda airport serves what Asian capital city?

QUIZ 32–33

33/3 ▶ What transport did the police mainly use in the TV show *CHiPs*?

33/4 ▶ The Sunda Strait separates Java from what other island?

33/5 ▶ Dramatist Eugene O'Neill was born in what country?

33/6 ▶ Which French novelist wrote *In Search of Lost Time*?

33/7 ▶ In song, what reindeer was told 'You'll go down in history'?

33/8 ▶ A lactoscope measures the quality of what liquid?

33/9 ▶ Harlech Castle was built by which king of England?

33/10 ▶ Kim Hunter first played chimpanzee Zira in what 1968 film?

33/11 ▶ What's the longest race in a women's heptathlon?

FINAL CHASE QUESTIONS

33/12 ▶ Where on the body are pumps worn?

33/13 ▶ Michelob is a brand of what alcoholic drink?

33/14 ▶ What's the capital of Jordan?

33/15 ▶ *Goodbye* was the 2013 greatest hits album by what boy band?

33/16 ▶ What is the official full name of the city of Stoke?

33/17 ▶ *Salute* is the 2013 album of which *X Factor* girl band?

33/18 ▶ Nell Gwyn was the mistress of which Stuart king?

33/19 ▶ What country's national anthem is 'La Brabançonne'?

33/20 ▶ What colour is Sonic the Hedgehog?

33/21 ▶ The Amritraj brothers represented India at what sport?

33/22 ▶ Non-ferrous refers to any metal except what?

33/23 ▶ Berkeley Castle is in what English county?

Final Chase Quiz 34

34/1 ▶ Who wrote the 1954 novel *Live and Let Die*?

34/2 ▶ The Alligator is native to Asia and what other continent?

34/3 ▶ Epinephrine is another name for what hormone?

34/4 ▶ What flavour ice cream is included in a peach Melba?

34/5 ▶ What year was a hit title for Prince?

34/6 ▶ The kiwi bird gets its name from what language?

FINAL CHASE QUESTIONS

34/7 ▶ What Dutch city is the home of the football team Vitesse?

34/8 ▶ Who's the father-in-law of Catherine, Duchess of Cambridge?

34/9 ▶ Who was the female agent in *Thunderbirds*?

34/10 ▶ The Eloi are a race of people in what H G Wells novel?

34/11 ▶ Both presidents called George Bush represented what party?

34/12 ▶ What is the capital of Ukraine?

34/13 ▶ What surname links famous British comedians Harry and Benny?

34/14 ▶ Hyperglycaemia is an excess of what sugar in the blood?

34/15 ▶ In 1675, John Flamsteed became the first what?

QUIZ 33–34

34/16 ▶ What marine mammal has species called 'harbour' and 'harp'?

34/17 ▶ Which actor played the title role in the film *The Graduate*?

34/18 ▶ Luxembourg has not entered what song contest since 1993?

34/19 ▶ Who directed the 2012 film *Savages*?

34/20 ▶ The word 'cosmic' derives from what ancient language?

34/21 ▶ Titleist is best known for making equipment for what sport?

34/22 ▶ What Mediterranean island was called 'Melita' by the Romans?

34/23 ▶ Jonny Mitchell is the headteacher in what TV documentary series?

Final Chase Quiz 35

35/1 ▶ 'Cavalier' is the French term for what chess piece?

35/2 ▶ What company published the *Harry Potter* novels in the UK?

35/3 ▶ What football club won its 13th Premier League title in 2013?

35/4 ▶ Who was the second American President to be impeached?

35/5 ▶ What sport featured in the Will Ferrell comedy *Semi-Pro*?

35/6 ▶ The SS *Great Western* was purpose-built to cross what ocean?

35/7 ▶ What video game's name comes from the Japanese for 'chomp'?

35/8 ▶ The mural painting *Guernica* is by which Spanish artist?

35/9 ▶ In what country was the political party Hezbollah founded?

35/10 ▶ In punctuation, how many dots make up a colon?

35/11 ▶ What artificial language has a name meaning 'one who hopes'?

35/12 ▶ What city is the capital of the Balearic Islands?

35/13 ▶ Which Beatle married Olivia Trinidad Arias?

35/14 ▶ In astronomy, what are red giants and white dwarves?

35/15 ▶ 'I do' is a phrase most associated with what ceremony?

35/16 ▶ The George Gershwin opera is *Porgy and...* who?

35/17 ▶ Who's the mother of US model Patrick Schwarzenegger?

35/18 ▶ Pay-as-you-earn taxation was introduced during which war?

35/19 ▶ 'Rolls' is a nickname for what make of car?

35/20 ▶ The Mozambique Channel is part of what ocean?

35/21 ▶ What does the S in SDTV stand for?

35/22 ▶ 'Boudoir' is a perfume by which British designer?

35/23 ▶ Which Scooby-Doo character has the catchphrase 'Puppy power'?

Final Chase Quiz 36

36/1 ▶ *The Hand of God* is a sculpture by which famous French artist?

36/2 ▶ What corporation broadcasts the 1Xtra urban radio station?

36/3 ▶ What does the medullary cavity of a human bone contain?

36/4 ▶ Adam Ant dressed as a highwayman in the video for what hit?

36/5 ▶ Bertha was the first wife of what *Jane Eyre* character?

36/6 ▶ What British city stands on the mouth of the River Tawe?

36/7 ▶ Fireworks were invented in which Asian country?

36/8 ▶ *Living for the Weekend* is a 2013 album by what girl group?

36/9 ▶ A tallith is a scarf worn at prayer in what religion?

36/10 ▶ What unit of computing information is abbreviated to TB?

36/11 ▶ Ben Nevis is in what country of the UK?

36/12 ▶ What colour is cartoon character Maggie Simpson's babygro?

36/13 ▶ Green Zebra is a variety of what salad ingredient?

36/14 ▶ Who won the Derby in 1954 as an 18-year-old?

FINAL CHASE QUESTIONS

36/15 ▷ What part of an Apollo spacecraft was known as the 'LM'?

36/16 ▷ Complete Gary Coleman's catchphrase 'What you talkin bout...'?

36/17 ▷ The Yellowstone River is in what country?

36/18 ▷ Who played Jane Foster in the 2013 film *Thor: The Dark World*?

36/19 ▷ What relation was Caligula to his successor Claudius?

36/20 ▷ A round in men's professional boxing lasts how many minutes?

36/21 ▷ Dolly Records is which country singer's own label?

36/22 ▷ The Crystal Palace was the first home of what military museum?

36/23 ▷ In the Narnia novels, who is the oldest Pevensie child?

Final Chase Quiz 37

37/1 ▶ Which Italian Renaissance master painted the 'Alba Madonna'?

37/2 ▶ Spies Guy Burgess and Kim Philby went to what university?

37/3 ▶ What's the second grand slam tennis tournament of the year?

37/4 ▶ CM in Roman numerals equals what number?

37/5 ▶ The alewife and shad belong to what fish family?

37/6 ▶ A Blue Peter flag features how many colours?

37/7 ▶ Actor Tom Cruise was born in what decade?

37/8 ▶ English scientist Dorothy Hodgkin won what Nobel Prize?

FINAL CHASE QUESTIONS

37/9 ▶ What type of pastry is used to make Beef Wellington?

37/10 ▶ Lawrence of Arabia died as a result of what incident?

37/11 ▶ In 2009, who became the oldest Briton to climb Everest?

37/12 ▶ Who hosts TV panel show *Was It Something I Said*?

37/13 ▶ The island of Corsica lies within what sea?

37/14 ▶ Elizabeth the First was the last monarch of what royal house?

37/15 ▶ Lamb's-tails are catkins from what tree?

37/16 ▶ Laurel and Hardy were both born in what century?

37/17 ▶ What did the Mormons officially abolish in 1890?

37/18 ▶ The sitcom *Dad's Army* was set in what war?

37/19 ▶ What style of coat does Paddington Bear wear?

37/20 ▶ Barolo is a red wine from what Italian region?

37/21 ▶ Soapstone is mainly composed of what mineral?

37/22 ▶ Who rode Nijinsky to a 1970 Derby victory?

37/23 ▶ *Domani* means 'tomorrow' in what language?

Final Chase Quiz 38

38/1 ▶ What colour is Marge Simpson's everyday dress?

38/2 ▶ Hatfield House is in which of the Home Counties?

38/3 ▶ The Bishops' Wars were in what century?

38/4 ▶ In Morse code, dash-dash-dash represents what vowel?

FINAL CHASE QUESTIONS

38/5 ▶ What tide occurs near the time of new and full moons?

38/6 ▶ What is pi rounded to the nearest whole number?

38/7 ▶ Scallops and oysters belong to what class of mollusc?

38/8 ▶ What soap features the fish and chip shop 'Beale's Plaice'?

38/9 ▶ Who led the Liberal party during its alliance with the SDP?

38/10 ▶ Who presents the TV series *Baking Mad*?

38/11 ▶ In teaching, ESL stands for 'English as a...' what?

38/12 ▶ Edward the Confessor was king in what century?

38/13 ▶ The Hayward Gallery is on the south bank of what river?

38/14 ▶ David Boreanaz plays Seeley Booth in what TV drama?

38/15 ▶ What animal is Tony in the Kellogg's adverts?

38/16 ▶ Which Liverpool footballer's nicknamed Stevie G?

38/17 ▶ What is Scotland's most northerly city?

38/18 ▶ In the film *Wall Street*, what meal is 'for wimps'?

38/19 ▶ What nationality was painter Raoul Dufy?

38/20 ▶ How many horse races make up America's Triple Crown?

38/21 ▶ Who had a 1990s hit with 'Ironic'?

38/22 ▶ Which king summoned the Long Parliament?

38/23 ▶ Egremont russet is a variety of what fruit?

Final Chase Quiz 39

39/1 ▶ What colour is the winter coat of a snowshoe hare?

39/2 ▶ The 'Devil's Cataract' is part of what African waterfall?

39/3 ▶ TV Series *Doc Martin* is set in what county?

39/4 ▶ What's the lowest female singing voice?

39/5 ▶ 'Mrs T' was a nickname of which politician?

39/6 ▶ The group Boyzone was formed in what country?

39/7 ▶ Vesper is another name for what planet?

39/8 ▶ David Beckham wore shirt number 32 playing for what club?

39/9 ▶ Which British actor was born Derek van den Bogaerde?

39/10 ▶ Which wartime general was created First Viscount of Alamein?

39/11 ▶ Fashion designer Gianni Versace was born in what country?

39/12 ▶ Which US Secretary of State was born in Bavaria in 1923?

39/13 ▶ What building on the Acropolis was designed by Ictinus?

39/14 ▶ What animal has the scientific name 'Canis lupus'?

39/15 ▶ Face Value in 1981 was whose first solo album?

39/16 ▶ The spice turmeric originated on what continent?

39/17 ▶ What 2005 film centres on the cowboys Ennis and Jack?

39/18 ▶ Alfred Lord Tennyson held what post longer than anyone else?

39/19 ▶ Who was the last king who had not been Prince of Wales?

39/20 ▶ In what board game do you get money for passing 'Go'?

39/21 ▶ In *EastEnders*, who was Dot Branning's son?

39/22 ▶ Which Ethiopian won two Olympic marathons in the 1960s?

39/23 ▶ Florenz Ziegfeld's 'follies' were based on which Parisian cabaret?

Final Chase Quiz 40

40/1 ▶ In the Bible, who was King of Judea when Jesus was born?

40/2 ▶ What fruit is the main ingredient of Heinz ketchup?

40/3 ▶ Pop group ABBA formed in what European capital city?

40/4 ▶ Bridesmaids are attendants at what traditional ceremony?

40/5 ▶ P Diddy and Puffy were alternative names for which rapper?

40/6 ▶ The official languages of Israel are Hebrew and what?

40/7 ▶ Which West Indian cricketer hit the first quadruple Test century?

40/8 ▶ What number is half a score?

40/9 ▶ Harvey's Cream Sherry is named after what British city?

40/10 ▶ Complete the title of the Billy Paul hit: 'Me and Mrs...' who?

40/11 ▶ Meriadoc Brandybuck was created by which author?

FINAL CHASE QUESTIONS

40/12 ▶ In what radio drama do Kenton and Jolene run the Bull pub?

40/13 ▶ Which famous artist was born in Manchester in 1887?

40/14 ▶ 'Being Boiled' was the first single by what Sheffield group?

40/15 ▶ What Czech car maker launched the 'Superb' model?

40/16 ▶ What 1972 disaster movie features an upturned ocean liner?

40/17 ▶ On an Italian menu, what is '*insalata*'?

40/18 ▶ Titus Livius was the full name of which Roman historian?

40/19 ▶ An ECG records the activity of what major organ?

40/20 ▶ What first name links the actors Burton, Harris and Dreyfuss?

40/21 ▶ The Gulf of Carpentaria is off the north coast of what country?

40/22 ▶ Nancy sings 'It's a Fine Life' in what Lionel Bart musical?

40/23 ▶ Beethoven was born in what modern day country?

CASH BUILDER

ANSWERS

![The Chase logo]

Cash Builder Quiz 1

1/1 ▶ Channel 4	1/9 ▶ Hercule Poirot
1/2 ▶ *Mamma Mia!*	1/10 ▶ Mark Wright
1/3 ▶ Virginia Wade	1/11 ▶ Photograph
1/4 ▶ Slow	1/12 ▶ Jeeves
1/5 ▶ Pope	1/13 ▶ Turkey
1/6 ▶ *Lyrical Ballads*	1/14 ▶ Europe
1/7 ▶ Conservative Party	1/15 ▶ Disneyland
1/8 ▶ Alton Towers	

Cash Builder Quiz 2

2/1 ▶ Valentines	2/6 ▶ *The Thieving Magpie*
2/2 ▶ *Neighbours*	2/7 ▶ Justin Bieber
2/3 ▶ Peron	2/8 ▶ Prince of Wales
2/4 ▶ Peter Crouch	2/9 ▶ Bourbon
2/5 ▶ Earth	2/10 ▶ Microsoft

2/11 ▶ Little Mix

2/12 ▶ Vilnius

2/13 ▶ Cadbury

2/14 ▶ Judi Dench

2/15 ▶ Savoy

Cash Builder Quiz 3

3/1 ▶ Autumn

3/2 ▶ *Made in Chelsea*

3/3 ▶ Eiffel Tower

3/4 ▶ Tony Blair

3/5 ▶ Henry the Eighth

3/6 ▶ Rock

3/7 ▶ 'Va Va Voom'

3/8 ▶ Equations

3/9 ▶ Ice Age

3/10 ▶ Romario

3/11 ▶ Hogwarts

3/12 ▶ Iberian

3/13 ▶ Chantelle Houghton

3/14 ▶ Dead Sea

3/15 ▶ A log

Cash Builder Quiz 4

4/1 ▶ Mary

4/2 ▶ 'Livin La Vida Loca'

4/3 ▶ Twickenham

4/4 ▶ April

4/5 ▶ Enrico Caruso

4/6 ▶ Power Rangers

4/7 ▶ Julius Caesar

4/8 ▶ Linen

4/9 ▶ Unicorn

4/10 ▶ Pocahontas

4/11 ▶ String

4/12 ▶ *Alice's Adventures in Wonderland*

4/13 ▶ 'Get Lucky'

4/14 ▶ Manic Street Preachers

4/15 ▶ Moon

Cash Builder Quiz 5

5/1 ▶ The Weasleys

5/2 ▶ France

5/3 ▶ *Malcolm in the Middle*

5/4 ▶ Darts

5/5 ▶ Hairy Bikers

5/6 ▶ Henry the Eighth

5/7 ▶ Fist

5/8 ▶ Air Force Two

5/9 ▶ *SHIELD*

5/10 ▶ Ballet

5/11 ▶ Dining Room

5/12 ▶ Rent

5/13 ▶ World War One

5/14 ▶ Pirates

5/15 ▶ 'I'm Too Sexy'

Cash Builder Quiz 6

6/1 ▶ Rabbits

6/2 ▶ Yellow

6/3 ▶ Female

6/4 ▶ Bletchley Park

6/5 ▶ Turner Prize

6/6 ▶ Heston Blumenthal

6/7 ▶ *Starlight Express*

6/8 ▶ Police

6/9 ▶ Victoria

6/10 ▶ Steve Wright

6/11 ▶ Fall

6/12 ▶ Nicholas the Second

6/13 ▶ Teeth

6/14 ▶ Manhattan

6/15 ▶ will.i.am

Cash Builder Quiz 7

7/1 ▶ IKEA

7/2 ▶ Conservative

7/3 ▶ Leonardo Da Vinci

7/4 ▶ Limescale

7/5 ▶ 1970s

7/6 ▶ *E.T: The Extra Terrestrial*

7/7 ▶ Jennifer Worth

7/8 ▶ Astronaut

7/9 ▶ Nike

7/10 ▶ Sherlock Holmes

7/11 ▶ RAF

7/12 ▶ Piglet

7/13 ▶ Houston

7/14 ▶ Elton John

7/15 ▶ War Horse

Cash Builder Quiz 8

8/1 ▶ Three

8/2 ▶ Thimble

8/3 ▶ Miranda Hart

8/4 ▶ Pink Lady

8/5 ▶ Tiffany

8/6 ▶ Snoop Dogg

8/7 ▶ Renoir

8/8 ▶ Blackpool

8/9 ▶ Miley Cyrus

8/10 ▶ Medici

8/11 ▶ Radio Caroline

8/12 ▶ Donkey

8/13 ▶ Yellow

8/14 ▶ Cupid

8/15 ▶ *Private Eye*

Cash Builder Quiz 9

9/1 ▶ Tony Jacklin

9/2 ▶ Rhine

9/3 ▶ The FA Cup

9/4 ▶ Twelve

9/5 ▶ Samuel L Jackson

9/6 ▶ Sausages

CASH BUILDER ANSWERS

9/7 ▶ *Super Mario*

9/8 ▶ Handed

9/9 ▶ Ravel

9/10 ▶ Steve Jobs

9/11 ▶ Reshuffle

9/12 ▶ Nicole Scherzinger

9/13 ▶ J R Hartley

9/14 ▶ Pope Francis

9/15 ▶ True Detective

Cash Builder Quiz 10

10/1 ▶ West Sussex

10/2 ▶ Lee Harvey Oswald

10/3 ▶ Brown

10/4 ▶ Two

10/5 ▶ Pac-Man

10/6 ▶ Pulp Fiction

10/7 ▶ George Galloway

10/8 ▶ Mowgli

10/9 ▶ Ronnie Corbett

10/10 ▶ Fast

10/11 ▶ *Blue Jasmine*

10/12 ▶ Bacchus

10/13 ▶ Full stop

10/14 ▶ Ellie Goulding

10/15 ▶ Henry the Eighth

THE CHASE

Cash Builder Quiz 11

11/1 ▶ Reverend W Awdry	11/9 ▶ *Trainspotting*
11/2 ▶ Penguin	11/10 ▶ Tardis
11/3 ▶ British Aerospace	11/11 ▶ Gary Rhodes
11/4 ▶ Winston Churchill	11/12 ▶ Chanel
11/5 ▶ *Avatar*	11/13 ▶ Galway
11/6 ▶ Brisbane	11/14 ▶ Rod Stewart
11/7 ▶ Head	11/15 ▶ Owl
11/8 ▶ John Legend	

Cash Builder Quiz 12

12/1 ▶ Foot	12/6 ▶ Rolex
12/2 ▶ Ireland	12/7 ▶ Ninety
12/3 ▶ *Quartet*	12/8 ▶ David Bowie
12/4 ▶ Magna Carta	12/9 ▶ *Moby-Dick*
12/5 ▶ Allotment	12/10 ▶ Israel

CASH BUILDER ANSWERS

12/11 ▶ 1950s

12/12 ▶ Twinkle Twinkle Little Star

12/13 ▶ Nokia

12/14 ▶ Drake

12/15 ▶ Sun

Cash Builder Quiz 13

13/1 ▶ X-Men

13/2 ▶ Jordan

13/3 ▶ Barack Obama

13/4 ▶ Plastic

13/5 ▶ AC Milan

13/6 ▶ Laugh

13/7 ▶ Belgium

13/8 ▶ Tony Hadley

13/9 ▶ Triple sec

13/10 ▶ Seven

13/11 ▶ Buttons

13/12 ▶ David Beckham

13/13 ▶ Game Boy

13/14 ▶ Cleopatra

13/15 ▶ Tanzania

Cash Builder Quiz 14

14/1 ▶ NASA

14/2 ▶ *Daggers*

14/3 ▶ Blue

14/4 ▶ Face

14/5 ▶ Toyota

14/6 ▶ Dean Martin

14/7 ▶ Gold

14/8 ▶ The Pope

14/9 ▶ 360

14/10 ▶ Henry Cooper

14/11 ▶ *A Child Called 'It'*

14/12 ▶ Crocodile

14/13 ▶ Icing sugar

14/14 ▶ Jeff

14/15 ▶ February

Cash Builder Quiz 15

15/1 ▶ Cut

15/2 ▶ Saudi Arabia

15/3 ▶ Heart

15/4 ▶ France

15/5 ▶ Salman Rushdie

15/6 ▶ Muhammad Ali

15/7 ▶ Mick Jagger

15/8 ▶ Culloden

15/9 ▶ Sunshine State

15/10 ▶ Bing Crosby

15/11 ▶ *Monkey Cage*

15/12 ▶ China

15/13 ▶ Sarah Storey

15/14 ▶ Titus Andronicus

15/15 ▶ Sailor

Cash Builder Quiz 16

16/1 ▶ Ming

16/2 ▶ Napoleon

16/3 ▶ Four

16/4 ▶ Patrick Swayze

16/5 ▶ The Eagle

16/6 ▶ Green

16/7 ▶ Notre Dame

16/8 ▶ Jeffrey Archer

16/9 ▶ Harmony

16/10 ▶ Toad

16/11 ▶ Budapest

16/12 ▶ Punt

16/13 ▶ Adolf Hitler

16/14 ▶ M

16/15 ▶ *Strangers On a Train*

Cash Builder Quiz 17

17/1 ▶ 'Eye of the Tiger'

17/2 ▶ Salvador Dalí

17/3 ▶ Queen Latifah

17/4 ▶ Cyprus

17/5 ▶ George W Bush

17/6 ▶ Tell

17/7 ▶ Ready to wear

17/8 ▶ 'He Ain't Heavy... He's My Brother'

17/9 ▶ Japan

17/10 ▶ Bourbon

17/11 ▶ *Napoleon Dynamite*

Cash Builder Quiz 18

Cash Builder Quiz 19

19/7 ▶ Cardiff City

19/8 ▶ Cluedo

19/9 ▶ Baileys

19/10 ▶ Coleridge

19/11 ▶ Louis Walsh

19/12 ▶ Elizabeth the First

19/13 ▶ Claudia Schiffer

19/14 ▶ Ceiling

19/15 ▶ Joaquin Phoenix

Cash Builder Quiz 20

20/1 ▶ Dollar

20/2 ▶ A flea

20/3 ▶ Oasis

20/4 ▶ Japan

20/5 ▶ Blood

20/6 ▶ Six

20/7 ▶ *Teachers*

20/8 ▶ Multiplex

20/9 ▶ Wayne Sleep

20/10 ▶ Barings

20/11 ▶ *Twilight Saga*

20/12 ▶ Buckingham Palace

20/13 ▶ Boat

20/14 ▶ Prince Harry

20/15 ▶ *Emmerdale*

Cash Builder Quiz 21

21/1 ▶ Wednesday

21/2 ▶ FBI

21/3 ▶ Kit Kat

21/4 ▶ '9 to 5'

21/5 ▶ UEFA

21/6 ▶ Flax

21/7 ▶ Sixty-four

21/8 ▶ Pole vault

21/9 ▶ Nelson Mandela

21/10 ▶ *Ice Age*

21/11 ▶ Crash helmets

21/12 ▶ Julien Macdonald

21/13 ▶ Dublin

21/14 ▶ *Oliver!*

21/15 ▶ *Mr Benn*

Cash Builder Quiz 22

22/1 ▶ *A Passage to India*

22/2 ▶ Ball

22/3 ▶ White House

22/4 ▶ Ola Jordan

22/5 ▶ Tokyo

22/6 ▶ Toll

22/7 ▶ *RoboCop*

22/8 ▶ Kellogg's

22/9 ▶ The Killers

22/10 ▶ Maisonette

CASH BUILDER ANSWERS

22/11 ▶ *Discworld*

22/12 ▶ Apes

22/13 ▶ The Beatles

22/14 ▶ Nelson Mandela

22/15 ▶ Theatres

Cash Builder Quiz 23

23/1 ▶ Sir Alex Ferguson

23/2 ▶ Jimmy Carr

23/3 ▶ Lord Kitchener

23/4 ▶ Wood

23/5 ▶ Sistine Chapel

23/6 ▶ Rafael Nadal

23/7 ▶ Seventeen

23/8 ▶ Abraham Lincoln

23/9 ▶ Ice

23/10 ▶ France

23/11 ▶ Harold Pinter

23/12 ▶ Royal Navy

23/13 ▶ The Mafia

23/14 ▶ James Franco

23/15 ▶ Bill Gates

Cash Builder Quiz 24

24/1 ▶ Hock

24/2 ▶ Rockies

24/3 ▶ *Have I Got News For You*

24/4 ▶ Duke of Wellington

24/5 ▶ Apostrophe

24/6 ▶ Yellowstone

24/7 ▶ Sean Paul

24/8 ▶ Roger Federer

24/9 ▶ Germany

24/10 ▶ HMS *Pinafore*

24/11 ▶ *A & E*

24/12 ▶ El Cid

24/13 ▶ Partnership

24/14 ▶ Uranus

24/15 ▶ *Buffy the Vampire Slayer*

Cash Builder Quiz 25

25/1 ▶ Party

25/2 ▶ David Dickinson

25/3 ▶ *The Three Musketeers*

25/4 ▶ Isle of Wight

25/5 ▶ Arsenal

25/6 ▶ *Hugo*

25/7 ▶ Coalition

25/8 ▶ *The Great Gatsby*

25/9 ▶ Basil

25/10 ▶ Fish

25/11 ▶ Rosetta Stone

25/12 ▶ Euro

25/13 ▶ *University Challenge*

25/14 ▶ *Love Me For A Reason*

25/15 ▶ B

CASH BUILDER ANSWERS

Cash Builder Quiz 26

26/1 ▶ Acorn

26/2 ▶ Reno

26/3 ▶ *The Fast Show*

26/4 ▶ Papa John's

26/5 ▶ Pink

26/6 ▶ *Who Framed Roger Rabbit*

26/7 ▶ Wife

26/8 ▶ Jedward

26/9 ▶ George the Third

26/10 ▶ Independence Party

26/11 ▶ Michael Jackson

26/12 ▶ Gallon

26/13 ▶ Richard Burton

26/14 ▶ Oprah Winfrey

26/15 ▶ Milka

Cash Builder Quiz 27

27/1 ▶ Vincent van Gogh

27/2 ▶ *Harry*

27/3 ▶ Brown

27/4 ▶ Hayley Williams

27/5 ▶ Conservative

27/6 ▶ Fiftieth

27/7 ▶ Philip Larkin

27/8 ▶ Horse racing

27/9 ▶ Hamlet

27/10 ▶ France

27/11 ▶ The Brits

27/12 ▶ Bushmills

27/13 ▶ Flowers

27/14 ▶ Safety pin

27/15 ▶ Kaiser Chiefs

Cash Builder Quiz 28

28/1 ▶ *Snow White*

28/2 ▶ Nebula

28/3 ▶ Steve Redgrave

28/4 ▶ Neil Diamond

28/5 ▶ Fidel Castro

28/6 ▶ The Tower of London

28/7 ▶ Road

28/8 ▶ Jumpers

28/9 ▶ Collins

28/10 ▶ Strings

28/11 ▶ *Life's Too Short*

28/12 ▶ Monarch

28/13 ▶ *Wonderful Wizard of Oz*

28/14 ▶ Robert

28/15 ▶ Miss Trunchbull

Cash Builder Quiz 29

29/1 ▶ Delta

29/2 ▶ Heinz

29/3 ▶ Andrew Ridgeley

29/4 ▶ Attila the Hen

29/5 ▶ W

29/6 ▶ Black

29/7 ▶ Martha Stewart

29/8 ▶ Scotland

29/9 ▶ Luigi

29/10 ▶ *Panic Room*

29/11 ▶ Coffee

29/12 ▶ Aswan High Dam

29/13 ▶ Liverpool

29/14 ▶ Happy Families

29/15 ▶ Jason Derulo

Cash Builder Quiz 30

30/1 ▶ One

30/2 ▶ James Bond

30/3 ▶ Go

30/4 ▶ Brazil

30/5 ▶ Tuscany

30/6 ▶ *Pride and Prejudice*

30/7 ▶ Andy Murray

30/8 ▶ Red

30/9 ▶ Antarctica

30/10 ▶ Milk

30/11 ▶ *Oliver!*

30/12 ▶ *The Catcher in the Rye*

30/13 ▶ Crosswords

30/14 ▶ 20th

30/15 ▶ Pink

THE CHASE

Cash Builder Quiz 31

31/1 ▶ Kennedy

31/2 ▶ The Forbidden City

31/3 ▶ Space

31/4 ▶ Fred Basset

31/5 ▶ Nando's

31/6 ▶ Southend

31/7 ▶ Franz Liszt

31/8 ▶ Apollo 13

31/9 ▶ Mary Berry

31/10 ▶ Fracking

31/11 ▶ Romans

31/12 ▶ *Fast and Furious Six*

31/13 ▶ Koran

31/14 ▶ Wales

31/15 ▶ L'Oréal

Cash Builder Quiz 32

32/1 ▶ Ed Sheeran

32/2 ▶ Lion

32/3 ▶ Dorothy

32/4 ▶ *Call The Midwife*

32/5 ▶ Gap year

32/6 ▶ Alexander the Great

32/7 ▶ Rugby union

32/8 ▶ Trunk

32/9 ▶ *The Great Gatsby*

32/10 ▶ Personal Best

32/11 ▶ Popeye	**32/14** ▶ Julia Roberts
32/12 ▶ Lacoste	**32/15** ▶ The Space Needle
32/13 ▶ Seven	

Cash Builder Quiz 33

33/1 ▶ Mexico	**33/9** ▶ Giant's Causeway
33/2 ▶ 12	**33/10** ▶ *Charlie and the Chocolate Factory*
33/3 ▶ Yahoo!	
33/4 ▶ Olly Murs	**33/11** ▶ Uncle
33/5 ▶ Impressionism	**33/12** ▶ George Clooney
33/6 ▶ Rice	**33/13** ▶ Persian Gulf
33/7 ▶ Golf	**33/14** ▶ Winter
33/8 ▶ Lorde	**33/15** ▶ Quality Street

Cash Builder Quiz 34

34/1 ▶ Prince Andrew	**34/4** ▶ Hans Christian Andersen
34/2 ▶ *Supermarket Sweep*	
34/3 ▶ Motherwell	**34/5** ▶ *Game of Thrones*

34/6 ▶ Mogul

34/7 ▶ Euro

34/8 ▶ Eisenhower

34/9 ▶ Pearl

34/10 ▶ Peggy Mitchell

34/11 ▶ Frying

34/12 ▶ Saturday

34/13 ▶ Cow pie

34/14 ▶ Bayeux Tapestry

34/15 ▶ Leprechaun

Cash Builder Quiz 35

35/1 ▶ Tennis

35/2 ▶ Priscilla Presley

35/3 ▶ Red

35/4 ▶ Brain

35/5 ▶ King's Road

35/6 ▶ 'Vienna'

35/7 ▶ William

35/8 ▶ The smooth

35/9 ▶ Superman

35/10 ▶ Steve Davis

35/11 ▶ Cluedo

35/12 ▶ British Airways

35/13 ▶ So Solid Crew

35/14 ▶ Catherine
of Aragon

35/15 ▶ Sherry

Cash Builder Quiz 36

36/1 ▶ Epcot

36/2 ▶ Mouth

36/3 ▶ Bronco

36/4 ▶ Gentleman

36/5 ▶ Theory of Relativity

36/6 ▶ The Flintstones

36/7 ▶ New Zealand

36/8 ▶ Dessert

36/9 ▶ Lester Piggott

36/10 ▶ Scarlett Johansson

36/11 ▶ St Swithin's Day

36/12 ▶ Tether

36/13 ▶ Cancer

36/14 ▶ Alfred Hitchcock

36/15 ▶ 'Babushka'

Cash Builder Quiz 37

37/1 ▶ St Paul's

37/2 ▶ Homophones

37/3 ▶ Sir Alex Ferguson

37/4 ▶ *Game of Thrones*

37/5 ▶ Karl Marx

37/6 ▶ Ridiculous

37/7 ▶ The Oval

37/8 ▶ Baseball cap

37/9 ▶ D A M

37/10 ▶ Photographer

37/11 ▶ Nylon

37/12 ▶ Car wash

37/13 ▶ Russia

37/14 ▶ Pluto

37/15 ▶ *New Tricks*

Cash Builder Quiz 38

38/1 ▶ Gerard Butler

38/2 ▶ Ronnie O'Sullivan

38/3 ▶ Surfing

38/4 ▶ Opaque

38/5 ▶ Spanish

38/6 ▶ China

38/7 ▶ *Narnia*

38/8 ▶ Famine

38/9 ▶ *Homefront*

38/10 ▶ Fleet Street

38/11 ▶ Einstein

38/12 ▶ Jamie Oliver

38/13 ▶ Trains

38/14 ▶ Narrow

38/15 ▶ Chicken tikka masala

Cash Builder Quiz 39

39/1 ▶ *Goldfinger*

39/2 ▶ Elbow

39/3 ▶ Orange

39/4 ▶ The Floss

39/5 ▶ Two

39/6 ▶ Gussie Moran

39/7 ▶ *The Sound of Music*	**39/12** ▶ Tornado
39/8 ▶ England	**39/13** ▶ Fern Britton
39/9 ▶ Taco	**39/14** ▶ Crook
39/10 ▶ Alcatraz	**39/15** ▶ White
39/11 ▶ Vampire	

Cash Builder Quiz 40

40/1 ▶ Apollo 10	**40/9** ▶ St Paul's Cathedral
40/2 ▶ 'I Will Survive'	**40/10** ▶ Mario
40/3 ▶ Vitamin D	**40/11** ▶ *Sweet Charity*
40/4 ▶ Pinocchio	**40/12** ▶ Virgo
40/5 ▶ Boxes	**40/13** ▶ *Derek*
40/6 ▶ Coffee	**40/14** ▶ Alec Douglas-Home
40/7 ▶ will.i.am	
40/8 ▶ Real Madrid	**40/15** ▶ Cinderella

HEAD TO HEAD

ANSWERS

Head to Head – The Governess Quiz 1

1/1 ▶ C	1/5 ▶ A*	1/9 ▶ A
1/2 ▶ A*	1/6 ▶ B	1/10 ▶ A
1/3 ▶ B	1/7 ▶ B	1/11 ▶ B*
1/4 ▶ C	1/8 ▶ C	1/12 ▶ B

Head to Head – The Governess Quiz 2

2/1 ▶ C	2/5 ▶ A	2/9 ▶ C
2/2 ▶ A	2/6 ▶ A	2/10 ▶ B*
2/3 ▶ B	2/7 ▶ A*	2/11 ▶ C*
2/4 ▶ C	2/8 ▶ B*	2/12 ▶ C*

Asterisks indicate the questions that the Chaser got wrong

Head to Head – The Governess Quiz 3

3/1 ▶ B	3/5 ▶ B*	3/9 ▶ C*
3/2 ▶ C	3/6 ▶ C	3/10 ▶ B
3/3 ▶ A	3/7 ▶ C	3/11 ▶ C
3/4 ▶ C*	3/8 ▶ A	3/12 ▶ C

Head to Head – The Governess Quiz 4

4/1 ▶ C	4/5 ▶ C	4/9 ▶ A
4/2 ▶ A	4/6 ▶ A	4/10 ▶ C
4/3 ▶ A	4/7 ▶ A*	4/11 ▶ B
4/4 ▶ B	4/8 ▶ C	4/12 ▶ A

Asterisks indicate the questions that the Chaser got wrong

![THE CHASE]

Head to Head – The Governess Quiz 5

5/1 ▶ A	5/5 ▶ A	5/9 ▶ B
5/2 ▶ B	5/6 ▶ C*	5/10 ▶ A
5/3 ▶ C	5/7 ▶ A	5/11 ▶ C*
5/4 ▶ A*	5/8 ▶ C	5/12 ▶ A

Head to Head – The Governess Quiz 6

6/1 ▶ B	6/5 ▶ C	6/9 ▶ B
6/2 ▶ B	6/6 ▶ A	6/10 ▶ C
6/3 ▶ B	6/7 ▶ C	6/11 ▶ C
6/4 ▶ C	6/8 ▶ A	6/12 ▶ A

Asterisks indicate the questions that the Chaser got wrong

Head to Head – The Governess Quiz 7

7/1 ▶ A	7/5 ▶ C	7/9 ▶ A
7/2 ▶ C	7/6 ▶ B*	7/10 ▶ B
7/3 ▶ A*	7/7 ▶ B	7/11 ▶ C
7/4 ▶ A	7/8 ▶ C	7/12 ▶ C*

Head to Head – The Governess Quiz 8

8/1 ▶ A	8/5 ▶ A	8/9 ▶ C
8/2 ▶ C	8/6 ▶ B*	8/10 ▶ B*
8/3 ▶ A	8/7 ▶ A	8/11 ▶ B
8/4 ▶ A	8/8 ▶ B	8/12 ▶ A*

Asterisks indicate the questions that the Chaser got wrong

Head to Head – The Governess Quiz 9

9/1 ▶ A   9/5 ▶ A   9/9 ▶ A

9/2 ▶ A   9/6 ▶ C   9/10 ▶ A

9/3 ▶ C   9/7 ▶ C*   9/11 ▶ C

9/4 ▶ C   9/8 ▶ B   9/12 ▶ A

Head to Head – The Governess Quiz 10

10/1 ▶ C*   10/5 ▶ C   10/9 ▶ A

10/2 ▶ A   10/6 ▶ B   10/10 ▶ A

10/3 ▶ A   10/7 ▶ C*   10/11 ▶ C

10/4 ▶ B*   10/8 ▶ B   10/12 ▶ C

Asterisks indicate the questions that the Chaser got wrong

Head to Head – The Beast Quiz 1

1/1 ▶ B	1/5 ▶ B	1/9 ▶ A
1/2 ▶ C	1/6 ▶ B	1/10 ▶ C*
1/3 ▶ B	1/7 ▶ A	1/11 ▶ C
1/4 ▶ A	1/8 ▶ B	1/12 ▶ B

Head to Head – The Beast Quiz 2

2/1 ▶ B	2/5 ▶ C*	2/9 ▶ C
2/2 ▶ B	2/6 ▶ C	2/10 ▶ B
2/3 ▶ B	2/7 ▶ C	2/11 ▶ B
2/4 ▶ C	2/8 ▶ A	2/12 ▶ A

Asterisks indicate the questions that the Chaser got wrong

Head to Head – The Beast Quiz 3

3/1 ▶ B   3/5 ▶ A*   3/9 ▶ B

3/2 ▶ A   3/6 ▶ C*   3/10 ▶ C

3/3 ▶ A   3/7 ▶ C   3/11 ▶ A

3/4 ▶ C   3/8 ▶ B   3/12 ▶ C

Head to Head – The Beast Quiz 4

4/1 ▶ A   4/5 ▶ B   4/9 ▶ B

4/2 ▶ B*   4/6 ▶ B   4/10 ▶ A

4/3 ▶ B   4/7 ▶ C   4/11 ▶ A

4/4 ▶ A   4/8 ▶ A   4/12 ▶ A

Asterisks indicate the questions that the Chaser got wrong

Head to Head – The Beast Quiz 5

5/1 ▶ B	5/5 ▶ A	5/9 ▶ A*
5/2 ▶ C	5/6 ▶ B*	5/10 ▶ C
5/3 ▶ C	5/7 ▶ B*	5/11 ▶ C
5/4 ▶ B*	5/8 ▶ C	5/12 ▶ C

Head to Head – The Beast Quiz 6

6/1 ▶ A	6/5 ▶ A	6/9 ▶ A
6/2 ▶ B*	6/6 ▶ B	6/10 ▶ A
6/3 ▶ C	6/7 ▶ B	6/11 ▶ B
6/4 ▶ C	6/8 ▶ A	6/12 ▶ C

Asterisks indicate the questions that the Chaser got wrong

Head to Head – The Beast Quiz 7

7/1 ▶ C*   7/5 ▶ B   7/9 ▶ C

7/2 ▶ C   7/6 ▶ A   7/10 ▶ B

7/3 ▶ B   7/7 ▶ B   7/11 ▶ A

7/4 ▶ C*   7/8 ▶ B   7/12 ▶ B*

Head to Head – The Beast Quiz 8

8/1 ▶ C   8/5 ▶ B   8/9 ▶ A*

8/2 ▶ C   8/6 ▶ C*   8/10 ▶ C

8/3 ▶ A*   8/7 ▶ C   8/11 ▶ C

8/4 ▶ A*   8/8 ▶ C   8/12 ▶ A

Asterisks indicate the questions that the Chaser got wrong

Head to Head – The Beast Quiz 9

9/1 ▶ C	9/5 ▶ C	9/9 ▶ B
9/2 ▶ A	9/6 ▶ A	9/10 ▶ B
9/3 ▶ C	9/7 ▶ A	9/11 ▶ A
9/4 ▶ A	9/8 ▶ C	9/12 ▶ A

Head to Head – The Beast Quiz 10

10/1 ▶ A	10/5 ▶ C*	10/9 ▶ C*
10/2 ▶ C	10/6 ▶ C	10/10 ▶ B
10/3 ▶ C	10/7 ▶ C	10/11 ▶ C*
10/4 ▶ C	10/8 ▶ A	10/12 ▶ B

Asterisks indicate the questions that the Chaser got wrong

Head to Head – The Sinnerman Quiz 1

1/1 ▶ B   1/5 ▶ C*   1/9 ▶ A

1/2 ▶ B   1/6 ▶ A   1/10 ▶ B

1/3 ▶ A   1/7 ▶ B*   1/11 ▶ A*

1/4 ▶ C   1/8 ▶ B   1/12 ▶ A

Head to Head – The Sinnerman Quiz 2

2/1 ▶ C*   2/5 ▶ B   2/9 ▶ A

2/2 ▶ B   2/6 ▶ C   2/10 ▶ B

2/3 ▶ C   2/7 ▶ A   2/11 ▶ A

2/4 ▶ B   2/8 ▶ A   2/12 ▶ B

Asterisks indicate the questions that the Chaser got wrong

Head to Head – The Sinnerman Quiz 3

3/1 ▶ C	3/5 ▶ C	3/9 ▶ B*
3/2 ▶ C*	3/6 ▶ B	3/10 ▶ B
3/3 ▶ B	3/7 ▶ A	3/11 ▶ A
3/4 ▶ A	3/8 ▶ A	3/12 ▶ A*

Head to Head – The Sinnerman Quiz 4

4/1 ▶ B	4/5 ▶ C*	4/9 ▶ B
4/2 ▶ B*	4/6 ▶ C	4/10 ▶ A
4/3 ▶ A	4/7 ▶ B	4/11 ▶ C
4/4 ▶ A	4/8 ▶ B	4/12 ▶ A

Asterisks indicate the questions that the Chaser got wrong

Head to Head – The Sinnerman Quiz 5

5/1 ▶ A	5/5 ▶ A	5/9 ▶ C*
5/2 ▶ A*	5/6 ▶ B*	5/10 ▶ C
5/3 ▶ A	5/7 ▶ B	5/11 ▶ A
5/4 ▶ C	5/8 ▶ C	5/12 ▶ B

Head to Head – The Sinnerman Quiz 6

6/1 ▶ A	6/5 ▶ A	6/9 ▶ A
6/2 ▶ A	6/6 ▶ C	6/10 ▶ C
6/3 ▶ B	6/7 ▶ A	6/11 ▶ B*
6/4 ▶ C*	6/8 ▶ A	6/12 ▶ C

Asterisks indicate the questions that the Chaser got wrong

Head to Head – The Sinnerman Quiz 7

7/1 ▶ C	7/5 ▶ C	7/9 ▶ B
7/2 ▶ C	7/6 ▶ A*	7/10 ▶ A
7/3 ▶ A	7/7 ▶ C	7/11 ▶ A
7/4 ▶ A*	7/8 ▶ C	7/12 ▶ B*

Head to Head – The Sinnerman Quiz 8

8/1 ▶ C	8/5 ▶ B	8/9 ▶ A
8/2 ▶ B	8/6 ▶ C	8/10 ▶ C
8/3 ▶ C	8/7 ▶ B*	8/11 ▶ C
8/4 ▶ A	8/8 ▶ C	8/12 ▶ C

Asterisks indicate the questions that the Chaser got wrong

Head to Head – The Sinnerman Quiz 9

9/1 ▶ A	9/5 ▶ B	9/9 ▶ B*
9/2 ▶ A	9/6 ▶ C	9/10 ▶ B
9/3 ▶ C*	9/7 ▶ A	9/11 ▶ C*
9/4 ▶ B	9/8 ▶ B	9/12 ▶ C

Head to Head – The Sinnerman Quiz 10

10/1 ▶ A	10/5 ▶ A*	10/9 ▶ C
10/2 ▶ C*	10/6 ▶ C	10/10 ▶ B
10/3 ▶ A	10/7 ▶ B	10/11 ▶ A
10/4 ▶ A	10/8 ▶ C*	10/12 ▶ A

Asterisks indicate the questions that the Chaser got wrong

HEAD-TO-HEAD ANSWERS

Head to Head – The Barrister Quiz 1

1/1 ▶ A	1/5 ▶ A	1/9 ▶ C*
1/2 ▶ C*	1/6 ▶ C	1/10 ▶ A
1/3 ▶ A	1/7 ▶ B	1/11 ▶ C*
1/4 ▶ B	1/8 ▶ B	1/12 ▶ B

Head to Head – The Barrister Quiz 2

2/1 ▶ B*	2/5 ▶ B	2/9 ▶ B
2/2 ▶ C*	2/6 ▶ A	2/10 ▶ A
2/3 ▶ B	2/7 ▶ A	2/11 ▶ C
2/4 ▶ A	2/8 ▶ A*	2/12 ▶ A

Asterisks indicate the questions that the Chaser got wrong

Head to Head – The Barrister Quiz 3

3/1 ▶ A	3/5 ▶ C*	3/9 ▶ C*
3/2 ▶ B	3/6 ▶ A	3/10 ▶ A
3/3 ▶ A	3/7 ▶ C	3/11 ▶ A
3/4 ▶ B	3/8 ▶ A	3/12 ▶ A

Head to Head – The Barrister Quiz 4

4/1 ▶ C	4/5 ▶ A	4/9 ▶ A*
4/2 ▶ C	4/6 ▶ C	4/10 ▶ C
4/3 ▶ C	4/7 ▶ B	4/11 ▶ B
4/4 ▶ C	4/8 ▶ A*	4/12 ▶ A

Asterisks indicate the questions that the Chaser got wrong

Head to Head – The Barrister Quiz 5

5/1 ▶ C	5/5 ▶ A	5/9 ▶ C
5/2 ▶ A	5/6 ▶ A	5/10 ▶ C
5/3 ▶ A*	5/7 ▶ C	5/11 ▶ A
5/4 ▶ B	5/8 ▶ A	5/12 ▶ B

Head to Head – The Barrister Quiz 6

6/1 ▶ A	6/5 ▶ B*	6/9 ▶ B
6/2 ▶ A*	6/6 ▶ A	6/10 ▶ A
6/3 ▶ C	6/7 ▶ A*	6/11 ▶ B
6/4 ▶ B*	6/8 ▶ C*	6/12 ▶ B*

Asterisks indicate the questions that the Chaser got wrong

Head to Head – The Barrister Quiz 7

7/1 ▶ B*	7/5 ▶ C	7/9 ▶ C*
7/2 ▶ A	7/6 ▶ A*	7/10 ▶ C
7/3 ▶ A*	7/7 ▶ A	7/11 ▶ A
7/4 ▶ B	7/8 ▶ A	7/12 ▶ A

Head to Head – The Barrister Quiz 8

8/1 ▶ C	8/5 ▶ C*	8/9 ▶ A*
8/2 ▶ C	8/6 ▶ B	8/10 ▶ C
8/3 ▶ A	8/7 ▶ A	8/11 ▶ B
8/4 ▶ B	8/8 ▶ B	8/12 ▶ B

Asterisks indicate the questions that the Chaser got wrong

Head to Head – The Barrister Quiz 9

9/1 ▶ B   9/5 ▶ A*   9/9 ▶ C*

9/2 ▶ A   9/6 ▶ C   9/10 ▶ A

9/3 ▶ C*   9/7 ▶ A   9/11 ▶ C

9/4 ▶ B   9/8 ▶ B   9/12 ▶ A

Head to Head – The Barrister Quiz 10

10/1 ▶ B   10/5 ▶ B   10/9 ▶ B

10/2 ▶ C   10/6 ▶ B   10/10 ▶ A

10/3 ▶ C   10/7 ▶ A   10/11 ▶ C

10/4 ▶ C   10/8 ▶ B   10/12 ▶ B

Asterisks indicate the questions that the Chaser got wrong

FINAL CHASE
ANSWERS

Final Chase Quiz 1

1/1 ▶ Trees

1/2 ▶ Edinburgh

1/3 ▶ *Hollyoaks*

1/4 ▶ Corfu

1/5 ▶ Five

1/6 ▶ Stephen King

1/7 ▶ Modelling

1/8 ▶ Three

1/9 ▶ *Wicked*

1/10 ▶ Cornea

1/11 ▶ Mouse

1/12 ▶ Uhura

1/13 ▶ Dreamliner

1/14 ▶ Roses

1/15 ▶ *The Nutcracker*

1/16 ▶ Latin

1/17 ▶ White

1/18 ▶ Russia

1/19 ▶ Two

1/20 ▶ Lincolnshire

1/21 ▶ Christopher Columbus

1/22 ▶ *Celebrity Big Brother*

1/23 ▶ *The Butler*

The target to beat the Chaser is 20

Final Chase Quiz 2

2/1 ▶ John

2/2 ▶ Fashion

2/3 ▶ Sun

2/4 ▶ Westlife

2/5 ▶ Francis Drake

2/6 ▶ *Fiddler on the Roof*

2/7 ▶ Chocolate

2/8 ▶ *Atlantis*

2/9 ▶ The Hatter's

2/10 ▶ Horse racing

2/11 ▶ Black

2/12 ▶ Mel C

2/13 ▶ Choux

2/14 ▶ Fish

2/15 ▶ Lacey Turner

2/16 ▶ Seven

2/17 ▶ Denmark

2/18 ▶ *101 Dalmatians*

2/19 ▶ Ballet

2/20 ▶ Squash

2/21 ▶ Sunglasses

2/22 ▶ Hampshire

2/23 ▶ Apple

FINAL CHASE QUIZ 1–2

The target to beat the Chaser is 19

Final Chase Quiz 3

3/1 ▶ 1066

3/2 ▶ *Ender's Game*

3/3 ▶ *The Gruffalo's Child*

3/4 ▶ Eighteen

3/5 ▶ Pacific

3/6 ▶ Tibia

3/7 ▶ Barack Obama

3/8 ▶ *Star Wars*

3/9 ▶ Mickey Mouse

3/10 ▶ Japan

3/11 ▶ 1930s

3/12 ▶ November

3/13 ▶ Nucleus

3/14 ▶ Coen brothers

3/15 ▶ Swimming

3/16 ▶ Q

3/17 ▶ Canada

3/18 ▶ Romulus and Remus

3/19 ▶ *Bad Education*

3/20 ▶ Nine

3/21 ▶ Leeds

3/22 ▶ Winston Churchill

3/23 ▶ *Silk*

The target to beat the Chaser is 21

Final Chase Quiz 4

4/1 ▶ *Macbeth*

4/2 ▶ Atlantic

4/3 ▶ Harvest

4/4 ▶ 'Radio Ga Ga'

4/5 ▶ Milan

4/6 ▶ Tolkien

4/7 ▶ Battersea

4/8 ▶ Seven

4/9 ▶ Prince Charles

4/10 ▶ *The Sound of Music*

4/11 ▶ Exodus

4/12 ▶ Reginald

4/13 ▶ Charlton Heston

4/14 ▶ Neck

4/15 ▶ One

4/16 ▶ Van Gogh

4/17 ▶ Green Day

4/18 ▶ Annie Oakley

4/19 ▶ Norwegian

4/20 ▶ Greek

4/21 ▶ Apple

4/22 ▶ Tenor

4/23 ▶ *Family Guy*

The target to beat the Chaser is 19

![The Chase logo]

Final Chase Quiz 5

5/1 ▶ Fourteen

5/2 ▶ Dog

5/3 ▶ J M Barrie

5/4 ▶ Transylvania

5/5 ▶ Natasha

5/6 ▶ Los Angeles

5/7 ▶ Salmon

5/8 ▶ Franklin Roosevelt

5/9 ▶ Enrique

5/10 ▶ Poland

5/11 ▶ Your Thumbs

5/12 ▶ *Cats*

5/13 ▶ Gemini

5/14 ▶ Seal

5/15 ▶ Netherlands

5/16 ▶ Columbia

5/17 ▶ Inches

5/18 ▶ Croatia

5/19 ▶ Sharks

5/20 ▶ American Civil War

5/21 ▶ J K Rowling

5/22 ▶ Montreal

5/23 ▶ Hundredweight

The target to beat the Chaser is 21

Final Chase Quiz 6

6/1 ▶ *The Archers*

6/2 ▶ Henry Knox

6/3 ▶ Thames

6/4 ▶ *Catch-22*

6/5 ▶ Saturn

6/6 ▶ Superman

6/7 ▶ New Jersey

6/8 ▶ Rugby Union

6/9 ▶ Lighthouse

6/10 ▶ Latin

6/11 ▶ Margaret Thatcher

6/12 ▶ Katy Perry

6/13 ▶ France

6/14 ▶ Green Gables

6/15 ▶ Lemon

6/16 ▶ 90

6/17 ▶ Helen

6/18 ▶ Tolkien

6/19 ▶ Asia

6/20 ▶ Alcohol

6/21 ▶ *Geordie Shore*

6/22 ▶ Democratic

6/23 ▶ Chelmsford

The target to beat the Chaser is 20

Final Chase Quiz 7

7/1 ▶ White

7/2 ▶ *Flowers in the Attic*

7/3 ▶ Mohammed Al Fayed

7/4 ▶ Bourbon

7/5 ▶ Frank Lloyd Wright

7/6 ▶ Luke

7/7 ▶ One

7/8 ▶ Wales

7/9 ▶ P L Travers

7/10 ▶ 500

7/11 ▶ Australia

7/12 ▶ *South Park*

7/13 ▶ Aintree

7/14 ▶ 1950s

7/15 ▶ Moscow

7/16 ▶ Broadway

7/17 ▶ NASA

7/18 ▶ The Buddha

7/19 ▶ Ireland

7/20 ▶ Michael Martin

7/21 ▶ Heineken

7/22 ▶ Jeeves

7/23 ▶ Athens

The target to beat the Chaser is 20

Final Chase Quiz 8

8/1 ▶ *La Cage aux Folles*	**8/13** ▶ Mark Cavendish
8/2 ▶ German	**8/14** ▶ Bones
8/3 ▶ Kian Egan	**8/15** ▶ The Sims
8/4 ▶ Wallace Collection	**8/16** ▶ Italy
8/5 ▶ Edinburgh	**8/17** ▶ Peter Phillips
8/6 ▶ St Paul	**8/18** ▶ Made in Chelsea
8/7 ▶ Two	**8/19** ▶ Vera Brittain
8/8 ▶ *The Jazz Singer*	**8/20** ▶ Brazil
8/9 ▶ Panama	**8/21** ▶ A P McCoy
8/10 ▶ Enamel	**8/22** ▶ Learning
8/11 ▶ *His Dark Materials*	**8/23** ▶ *Tender is the Night*
8/12 ▶ Elton John	

The target to beat the Chaser is 19

Final Chase Quiz 9

9/1 ▶ Roman	**9/13** ▶ Comics
9/2 ▶ Boar	**9/14** ▶ The North Sea
9/3 ▶ Alexander Pope	**9/15** ▶ German
9/4 ▶ Relativity	**9/16** ▶ M5
9/5 ▶ Cardiff	**9/17** ▶ Julian Fellowes
9/6 ▶ *The Wizard of Oz*	**9/18** ▶ Invisible Woman
9/7 ▶ Noël Coward	**9/19** ▶ Yellow
9/8 ▶ Boxing	**9/20** ▶ Three
9/9 ▶ Spain	**9/21** ▶ *Keeping Up Appearances*
9/10 ▶ Edward the Third	**9/22** ▶ Exodus
9/11 ▶ Orson	**9/23** ▶ Martin
9/12 ▶ Swiss	

The target to beat the Chaser is 19

Final Chase Quiz 10

10/1 ▶ Lanzarote

10/2 ▶ Fletcher

10/3 ▶ *Moby-Dick*

10/4 ▶ Police Department

10/5 ▶ Feet

10/6 ▶ Chess

10/7 ▶ Roses

10/8 ▶ Denmark

10/9 ▶ Racecourse

10/10 ▶ Clio

10/11 ▶ Italy

10/12 ▶ Dinosaurs

10/13 ▶ Jimmy Fallon

10/14 ▶ Brazil

10/15 ▶ Westminster Abbey

10/16 ▶ 1980s

10/17 ▶ Sophie Kinsella

10/18 ▶ San Francisco

10/19 ▶ *Indiana Jones and the Temple of Doom*

10/20 ▶ Chopsticks

10/21 ▶ Saturn

10/22 ▶ Poker

10/23 ▶ Baseball

The target to beat the Chaser is 18

THE CHASE

Final Chase Quiz 11

11/1 ▶ Transport	**11/13** ▶ Jo Nesbo
11/2 ▶ Rod Stewart	**11/14** ▶ *Donnie Darko*
11/3 ▶ *The Grapes of Wrath*	**11/15** ▶ Lancelot
11/4 ▶ Zebra	**11/16** ▶ Edward the Eighth
11/5 ▶ Beethoven	**11/17** ▶ Lester Piggott
11/6 ▶ Obituary	**11/18** ▶ Dorothy
11/7 ▶ Las Vegas	**11/19** ▶ Five
11/8 ▶ The Verve	**11/20** ▶ Eleanor
11/9 ▶ World War Two	**11/21** ▶ Egypt
11/10 ▶ *Henry the Eighth*	**11/22** ▶ Stink
11/11 ▶ Rugby League	**11/23** ▶ Cricket
11/12 ▶ Hoover Dam	

The target to beat the Chaser is 19

Final Chase Quiz 12

12/1 ▶ V

12/2 ▶ Alfred Hitchcock

12/3 ▶ Deck-chair

12/4 ▶ Kingdom

12/5 ▶ Dan Aykroyd

12/6 ▶ Derek Robinson

12/7 ▶ *Oliver Twist*

12/8 ▶ Monte Carlo

12/9 ▶ 1990s

12/10 ▶ Neil Armstrong

12/11 ▶ Dame Edna Everage

12/12 ▶ Susan Boyle

12/13 ▶ Airbus

12/14 ▶ Anastasia

12/15 ▶ Hop

12/16 ▶ Holy Spirit

12/17 ▶ Portable

12/18 ▶ Wrestling

12/19 ▶ Margery Daw

12/20 ▶ Canal

12/21 ▶ Paris

12/22 ▶ *The Big Breakfast*

12/23 ▶ South Africa

The target to beat the Chaser is 20

Final Chase Quiz 13

13/1 ▶ Gucci

13/2 ▶ White

13/3 ▶ 1970s

13/4 ▶ Tony Soprano

13/5 ▶ Head

13/6 ▶ Four

13/7 ▶ Money

13/8 ▶ India

13/9 ▶ Sega

13/10 ▶ Swimming

13/11 ▶ The ear

13/12 ▶ Niece

13/13 ▶ Argentina

13/14 ▶ Champagne

13/15 ▶ Trafalgar Square

13/16 ▶ Dennis Hopper

13/17 ▶ Louis the Fourteenth

13/18 ▶ Dog

13/19 ▶ World War Two

13/20 ▶ Triangle

13/21 ▶ *Wicked*

13/22 ▶ Atlantic Ocean

13/23 ▶ Jocky Wilson

The target to beat the Chaser is 17

Final Chase Quiz 14

14/1 ▶ Time		**14/13** ▶ Fifty-four
14/2 ▶ Russia		**14/14** ▶ The Prodigy
14/3 ▶ Apple		**14/15** ▶ Athletics
14/4 ▶ Andrew		**14/16** ▶ Bruno Mars
14/5 ▶ Tina Turner		**14/17** ▶ Triton
14/6 ▶ Bangkok		**14/18** ▶ Melanie
14/7 ▶ Superman		**14/19** ▶ *Call of Duty*
14/8 ▶ Beer		**14/20** ▶ Tobacco
14/9 ▶ *The Return of the King*		**14/21** ▶ Tom Kerridge
14/10 ▶ The Beautiful South		**14/22** ▶ Sean
14/11 ▶ Asia		**14/23** ▶ Alex Ferguson
14/12 ▶ *The Lion King*		

The target to beat the Chaser is 19

Final Chase Quiz 15

15/1 ▶ Nuts

15/2 ▶ Nicolas Sarkozy

15/3 ▶ Union J

15/4 ▶ Kipper

15/5 ▶ Seville

15/6 ▶ *The Commitments*

15/7 ▶ *The Flintstones*

15/8 ▶ Rome

15/9 ▶ New Zealand

15/10 ▶ 57

15/11 ▶ *Cats*

15/12 ▶ David Guetta

15/13 ▶ 72

15/14 ▶ Miuccia Prada

15/15 ▶ Beetle

15/16 ▶ Leonardo DiCaprio

15/17 ▶ Belgium

15/18 ▶ Fidel Castro

15/19 ▶ Taurus

15/20 ▶ Curriculum Vitae

15/21 ▶ Seventeenth

15/22 ▶ Macbeth

15/23 ▶ Butterfly

The target to beat the Chaser is 20

Final Chase Quiz 16

16/1 ▶ *Geordie Shore*

16/2 ▶ Beatrix Potter

16/3 ▶ *High School Musical*

16/4 ▶ June

16/5 ▶ Sudoku

16/6 ▶ Marie Antoinette

16/7 ▶ Red

16/8 ▶ London

16/9 ▶ Sushi

16/10 ▶ *Witness*

16/11 ▶ Florence Nightingale

16/12 ▶ Greek

16/13 ▶ Graceland

16/14 ▶ Mickey Spillane

16/15 ▶ 1970s

16/16 ▶ Little Mix

16/17 ▶ Swimming

16/18 ▶ 27

16/19 ▶ Gateshead

16/20 ▶ Cain

16/21 ▶ Robert Englund

16/22 ▶ Sword

16/23 ▶ The eye

The target to beat the Chaser is 19

Final Chase Quiz 17

17/1 ▶ Diesel

17/2 ▶ A gift horse

17/3 ▶ One Direction

17/4 ▶ Vladimir

17/5 ▶ July

17/6 ▶ Cwmbrân

17/7 ▶ Jam

17/8 ▶ Beach volleyball

17/9 ▶ Somerset

17/10 ▶ *The Bourne Legacy*

17/11 ▶ One hundred

17/12 ▶ Heracles

17/13 ▶ Cornwall

17/14 ▶ Valentino

17/15 ▶ Skin

17/16 ▶ Westlife

17/17 ▶ Stevie Smith

17/18 ▶ Scotland

17/19 ▶ Daniel Day-Lewis

17/20 ▶ Asia

17/21 ▶ Daft Punk

17/22 ▶ Orange

17/23 ▶ Ear

The target to beat the Chaser is 21

Final Chase Quiz 18

18/1 ▶ *Coppelia*

18/2 ▶ Cricket

18/3 ▶ Nile

18/4 ▶ Two

18/5 ▶ Richie Cunningham

18/6 ▶ Alderney

18/7 ▶ Alton Towers

18/8 ▶ Exodus

18/9 ▶ Sydney Harbour Bridge

18/10 ▶ Dutch

18/11 ▶ John Cusack

18/12 ▶ Radius

18/13 ▶ *The Tempest*

18/14 ▶ Chief Petty Officer

18/15 ▶ Lebanon

18/16 ▶ Antarctica

18/17 ▶ Aaron Paul

18/18 ▶ Black and white

18/19 ▶ Germany

18/20 ▶ Richard Rogers

18/21 ▶ *The Good Life*

18/22 ▶ March

18/23 ▶ Seven

The target to beat the Chaser is 19

Final Chase Quiz 19

19/1 ▶ Colonel Gaddafi

19/2 ▶ Arctic Monkeys

19/3 ▶ *Chitty Chitty Bang Bang*

19/4 ▶ Boxing

19/5 ▶ *The Fast Show*

19/6 ▶ World War Two

19/7 ▶ Lord Byron

19/8 ▶ Spanish

19/9 ▶ Manhattan

19/10 ▶ Sting

19/11 ▶ Thymus

19/12 ▶ Bartholomew

19/13 ▶ *Heat*

19/14 ▶ Lord Denning

19/15 ▶ 66

19/16 ▶ Lily Allen

19/17 ▶ Sheep

19/18 ▶ Quartermaster-General

19/19 ▶ Venus

19/20 ▶ The Everglades

19/21 ▶ *Aida*

19/22 ▶ Three

19/23 ▶ Adolf Hitler

The target to beat the Chaser is 18

Final Chase Quiz 20

20/1 ▶ Buckingham Palace

20/2 ▶ Roe

20/3 ▶ Roman

20/4 ▶ Africa

20/5 ▶ *The Crimson Field*

20/6 ▶ Polperro

20/7 ▶ China

20/8 ▶ Modelling

20/9 ▶ Nine

20/10 ▶ Mars

20/11 ▶ Italy

20/12 ▶ 19th

20/13 ▶ Wiltshire

20/14 ▶ *A Fish Called Wanda*

20/15 ▶ Spain

20/16 ▶ Toadstool

20/17 ▶ Belgium

20/18 ▶ Sven-Göran Eriksson

20/19 ▶ Light

20/20 ▶ Stewart Lee

20/21 ▶ Manchester

20/22 ▶ Irish wolfhound

20/23 ▶ French

The target to beat the Chaser is 20

Final Chase Quiz 21

21/1 ▶ Trisha Goddard

21/2 ▶ Nine

21/3 ▶ Will Smith

21/4 ▶ Spanish

21/5 ▶ Berlin

21/6 ▶ Pete Townshend

21/7 ▶ Beluga

21/8 ▶ Greece

21/9 ▶ *Grey's Anatomy*

21/10 ▶ 19th

21/11 ▶ Franz Liszt

21/12 ▶ Embroidery

21/13 ▶ Alexander the Great

21/14 ▶ Poet Laureate

21/15 ▶ Tomato

21/16 ▶ *Peep Show*

21/17 ▶ Magnus Magnusson

21/18 ▶ *Desert Island Discs*

21/19 ▶ Yellow

21/20 ▶ Caribbean Sea

21/21 ▶ Rudimental

21/22 ▶ The Sun

21/23 ▶ Vein

The target to beat the Chaser is 19

Final Chase Quiz 22

22/1 ▶ London	**22/13** ▶ Account
22/2 ▶ Hundred Years' War	**22/14** ▶ Banana
22/3 ▶ *Mr Bean's Holiday*	**22/15** ▶ Red
22/4 ▶ Memphis	**22/16** ▶ Cornwall
22/5 ▶ Bird	**22/17** ▶ Elaine Paige
22/6 ▶ Tennis	**22/18** ▶ Copper
22/7 ▶ Cairngorms	**22/19** ▶ Table tennis
22/8 ▶ Rio Grande	**22/20** ▶ Tempo
22/9 ▶ James Watson	**22/21** ▶ Anchovies
22/10 ▶ Bolshoi	**22/22** ▶ Wishbone
22/11 ▶ *Home and Away*	**22/23** ▶ Virginia
22/12 ▶ Oysters	

The target to beat the Chaser is 19

Final Chase Quiz 23

23/1 ▶ Germany

23/2 ▶ Elliott

23/3 ▶ September

23/4 ▶ Africa

23/5 ▶ 18th century

23/6 ▶ Fringe

23/7 ▶ Paul Young

23/8 ▶ Panthers

23/9 ▶ Limestone

23/10 ▶ Greek

23/11 ▶ Wine

23/12 ▶ Radio 4

23/13 ▶ Norway

23/14 ▶ Frankenstein

23/15 ▶ George Harrison

23/16 ▶ Five

23/17 ▶ Edelweiss

23/18 ▶ April

23/19 ▶ Spanish

23/20 ▶ Jules Verne

23/21 ▶ Monkey

23/22 ▶ Poker

23/23 ▶ Lawn Tennis Association

The target to beat the Chaser is 18

Final Chase Quiz 24

24/1 ▶	Ganges		24/12 ▶	Ireland
24/2 ▶	James Blunt		24/13 ▶	Rockies
24/3 ▶	Ballet		24/14 ▶	White
24/4 ▶	Mob		24/15 ▶	Fibula
24/5 ▶	Dada		24/16 ▶	Baltic
24/6 ▶	Scotland		24/17 ▶	Bowler hats
24/7 ▶	Zulu		24/18 ▶	Barack Obama
24/8 ▶	Vodka		24/19 ▶	'Imagine'
24/9 ▶	Arnold Schwarzenegger		24/20 ▶	Canada
			24/21 ▶	Cream of Tartar
24/10 ▶	Ten		24/22 ▶	Heptathlon
24/11 ▶	Manchester		24/23 ▶	Piano

The target to beat the Chaser is 20

Final Chase Quiz 25

The target to beat the Chaser is 19

Final Chase Quiz 26

26/1 ▶ *The Birth of Venus*

26/2 ▶ Spain

26/3 ▶ *Hercules*

26/4 ▶ Buddhism

26/5 ▶ Paddington

26/6 ▶ Catherine Parr

26/7 ▶ Kylie Minogue

26/8 ▶ Pacific Ocean

26/9 ▶ Rodents

26/10 ▶ John F Kennedy

26/11 ▶ Thirty

26/12 ▶ *Coronation Street*

26/13 ▶ Carlisle United

26/14 ▶ Chinese

26/15 ▶ Gucci

26/16 ▶ Horse

26/17 ▶ *2 Point 4 Children*

26/18 ▶ *Sunset Boulevard*

26/19 ▶ Cape Canaveral

26/20 ▶ Edinburgh

26/21 ▶ James Blunt

26/22 ▶ Scarlett O'Hara

26/23 ▶ David

The target to beat the Chaser is 20

Final Chase Quiz 27

27/1 ▶ Indian

27/2 ▶ Four

27/3 ▶ Kirstie Allsopp

27/4 ▶ 19th

27/5 ▶ Football

27/6 ▶ Quicker

27/7 ▶ Chess

27/8 ▶ Haemoglobin

27/9 ▶ New York

27/10 ▶ Carol Ann Duffy

27/11 ▶ Caves

27/12 ▶ Ugly Sisters

27/13 ▶ Elgin marbles

27/14 ▶ The Sun

27/15 ▶ George the Fifth

27/16 ▶ Barbra Streisand

27/17 ▶ Ice-cream

27/18 ▶ Avalon

27/19 ▶ *Ghostbusters*

27/20 ▶ New Mexico

27/21 ▶ Honeymoon

27/22 ▶ Tiger

27/23 ▶ Scott Joplin

The target to beat the Chaser is 21

Final Chase Quiz 28

28/1 ▶ Neil Armstrong	**28/12** ▶ U2
28/2 ▶ Italy	**28/13** ▶ Portugal
28/3 ▶ John Lennon	**28/14** ▶ Pound
28/4 ▶ Hinduism	**28/15** ▶ Princess Anne
28/5 ▶ Two	**28/16** ▶ Avocado
28/6 ▶ Tokyo	**28/17** ▶ Thomas
28/7 ▶ Foster's	**28/18** ▶ Fourteenth Century
28/8 ▶ *The Pilgrim's Progress*	**28/19** ▶ *A Question of Sport*
	28/20 ▶ Africa
28/9 ▶ Pegasus	**28/21** ▶ Robbie Williams
28/10 ▶ Sean Penn	**28/22** ▶ Zeus
28/11 ▶ Yangon	**28/23** ▶ Dynamo Kiev

The target to beat the Chaser is 20

Final Chase Quiz 29

29/1 ▶ Theatre	**29/13** ▶ Westminster Cathedral
29/2 ▶ Wrestling	
29/3 ▶ Robert	**29/14** ▶ Glasgow
29/4 ▶ Australia	**29/15** ▶ Wellington
29/5 ▶ *Watership Down*	**29/16** ▶ Potatoes
29/6 ▶ *Chess*	**29/17** ▶ California
29/7 ▶ Spandau Ballet	**29/18** ▶ Captain Queeg
29/8 ▶ Buzz Aldrin	**29/19** ▶ Ovaries
29/9 ▶ Portugal	**29/20** ▶ Paris Hilton
29/10 ▶ Henrik Ibsen	**29/21** ▶ Find
29/11 ▶ Alvin Stardust	**29/22** ▶ Secretary-General
29/12 ▶ 1990s	**29/23** ▶ Polyester

The target to beat the Chaser is 19

Final Chase Quiz 30

30/1 ▶ Love

30/2 ▶ Mother Teresa

30/3 ▶ Breast

30/4 ▶ South America

30/5 ▶ Hirohito

30/6 ▶ *Driving Miss Daisy*

30/7 ▶ Dolce & Gabbana

30/8 ▶ Inverness

30/9 ▶ Fish

30/10 ▶ Final Fantasy

30/11 ▶ Texas

30/12 ▶ *Time*

30/13 ▶ Nazi

30/14 ▶ Greece

30/15 ▶ Lance Armstrong

30/16 ▶ Henry

30/17 ▶ Her Britannic Majesty

30/18 ▶ Sailing

30/19 ▶ Penguins

30/20 ▶ Green

30/21 ▶ Nokia

30/22 ▶ 19th

30/23 ▶ Glasgow

The target to beat the Chaser is 20

Final Chase Quiz 31

31/1 ▶ *Aladdin*

31/2 ▶ James Cook

31/3 ▶ Denmark

31/4 ▶ N

31/5 ▶ Loyd Grossman

31/6 ▶ Pound foolish

31/7 ▶ Canis Major

31/8 ▶ Argentina

31/9 ▶ Julia Roberts

31/10 ▶ John Galsworthy

31/11 ▶ Calvin Klein

31/12 ▶ Physics

31/13 ▶ Pacific Ocean

31/14 ▶ Pauline McLynn

31/15 ▶ 150

31/16 ▶ Ludwig van Beethoven

31/17 ▶ Gertrude Shilling

31/18 ▶ Roy Orbison

31/19 ▶ *Around the World in 80 Days*

31/20 ▶ *The Flintstones*

31/21 ▶ Yellow

31/22 ▶ Winter

31/23 ▶ Car

The target to beat the Chaser is 19

Final Chase Quiz 32

32/1 ▷ George the Fifth

32/2 ▷ The Light Brigade

32/3 ▷ St Kitts

32/4 ▷ Pierce Brosnan

32/5 ▷ Italian

32/6 ▷ Schnauzer

32/7 ▷ 18th

32/8 ▷ Taggart

32/9 ▷ *Salomé*

32/10 ▷ Manchester United

32/11 ▷ Prado

32/12 ▷ Two

32/13 ▷ Diana Vickers

32/14 ▷ One-twelfth

32/15 ▷ White

32/16 ▷ Aunt

32/17 ▷ Josh Groban

32/18 ▷ Lima

32/19 ▷ Sarah Jane Smith

32/20 ▷ Spain

32/21 ▷ Madagascar

32/22 ▷ Harry S Truman

32/23 ▷ Almond

The target to beat the Chaser is 20

Final Chase Quiz 33

33/1 ▶ Earth, Wind and Fire

33/2 ▶ Tokyo

33/3 ▶ Motorcycles

33/4 ▶ Sumatra

33/5 ▶ USA

33/6 ▶ Marcel Proust

33/7 ▶ Rudolph

33/8 ▶ Milk

33/9 ▶ Edward the First

33/10 ▶ *Planet of the Apes*

33/11 ▶ 800 metres

33/12 ▶ Feet

33/13 ▶ Beer

33/14 ▶ Amman

33/15 ▶ JLS

33/16 ▶ Stoke-on-Trent

33/17 ▶ Little Mix

33/18 ▶ Charles the Second

33/19 ▶ Belgium

33/20 ▶ Blue

33/21 ▶ Tennis

33/22 ▶ Iron

33/23 ▶ Gloucestershire

The target to beat the Chaser is 21

Final Chase Quiz 34

34/1 ▶ Ian Fleming

34/2 ▶ North America

34/3 ▶ Adrenaline

34/4 ▶ Vanilla

34/5 ▶ 1999

34/6 ▶ Maori

34/7 ▶ Arnhem

34/8 ▶ Prince Charles

34/9 ▶ Lady Penelope

34/10 ▶ *The Time Machine*

34/11 ▶ Republican

34/12 ▶ Kiev

34/13 ▶ Hill

34/14 ▶ Glucose

34/15 ▶ Astronomer Royal

34/16 ▶ Seal

34/17 ▶ Dustin Hoffman

34/18 ▶ Eurovision

34/19 ▶ Oliver Stone

34/20 ▶ Greek

34/21 ▶ Golf

34/22 ▶ Malta

34/23 ▶ *Educating Yorkshire*

The target to beat the Chaser is 18

Final Chase Quiz 35

35/1 ▶ Knight

35/2 ▶ Bloomsbury

35/3 ▶ Manchester United

35/4 ▶ Bill Clinton

35/5 ▶ Basketball

35/6 ▶ Atlantic

35/7 ▶ Pac-Man

35/8 ▶ Picasso

35/9 ▶ Lebanon

35/10 ▶ Two

35/11 ▶ Esperanto

35/12 ▶ Palma

35/13 ▶ George Harrison

35/14 ▶ Stars

35/15 ▶ Marriage

35/16 ▶ *Bess*

35/17 ▶ Maria Shriver

35/18 ▶ World War Two

35/19 ▶ Rolls-Royce

35/20 ▶ Indian

35/21 ▶ Standard

35/22 ▶ Vivienne Westwood

35/23 ▶ Scrappy-Doo

The target to beat the Chaser is 19

Final Chase Quiz 36

36/1 ▶ Rodin

36/2 ▶ BBC

36/3 ▶ Bone marrow

36/4 ▶ 'Stand and Deliver'

36/5 ▶ Mr Rochester

36/6 ▶ Swansea

36/7 ▶ China

36/8 ▶ The Saturdays

36/9 ▶ Judaism

36/10 ▶ Terabyte

36/11 ▶ Scotland

36/12 ▶ Blue

36/13 ▶ Tomato

36/14 ▶ Lester Piggott

36/15 ▶ Lunar Module

36/16 ▶ Willis

36/17 ▶ United States

36/18 ▶ Natalie Portman

36/19 ▶ Nephew

36/20 ▶ Three

36/21 ▶ Dolly Parton

36/22 ▶ Imperial War Museum

36/23 ▶ Peter

The target to beat the Chaser is 19

Final Chase Quiz 37

37/1 ▶ Raphael

37/2 ▶ Cambridge

37/3 ▶ French Open

37/4 ▶ 900

37/5 ▶ Herring

37/6 ▶ Two

37/7 ▶ 1960s

37/8 ▶ Chemistry

37/9 ▶ Puff

37/10 ▶ Motorcycle accident

37/11 ▶ Sir Ranulph Fiennes

37/12 ▶ David Mitchell

37/13 ▶ Mediterranean

37/14 ▶ Tudor

37/15 ▶ Hazel

37/16 ▶ Nineteenth

37/17 ▶ Polygamy

37/18 ▶ World War Two

37/19 ▶ Duffle coat

37/20 ▶ Piedmont

37/21 ▶ Talc

37/22 ▶ Lester Piggott

37/23 ▶ Italian

The target to beat the Chaser is 20

Final Chase Quiz 38

38/1 ▶ Green

38/2 ▶ Hertfordshire

38/3 ▶ 17th

38/4 ▶ O

38/5 ▶ Spring tide

38/6 ▶ Three

38/7 ▶ Bivalvia

38/8 ▶ *EastEnders*

38/9 ▶ David Steel

38/10 ▶ Eric Lanlard

38/11 ▶ Second Language

38/12 ▶ 11th

38/13 ▶ Thames

38/14 ▶ *Bones*

38/15 ▶ Tiger

38/16 ▶ Steven Gerrard

38/17 ▶ Inverness

38/18 ▶ Lunch

38/19 ▶ French

38/20 ▶ Three

38/21 ▶ Alanis Morissette

38/22 ▶ Charles the First

38/23 ▶ Apple

The target to beat the Chaser is 20

Final Chase Quiz 39

39/1 ▶ White

39/2 ▶ Victoria Falls

39/3 ▶ Cornwall

39/4 ▶ Contralto

39/5 ▶ Margaret Thatcher

39/6 ▶ Ireland

39/7 ▶ Venus

39/8 ▶ AC Milan

39/9 ▶ Dirk Bogarde

39/10 ▶ Montgomery

39/11 ▶ Italy

39/12 ▶ Henry Kissinger

39/13 ▶ The Parthenon

39/14 ▶ Wolf

39/15 ▶ Phil Collins

39/16 ▶ Asia

39/17 ▶ *Brokeback Mountain*

39/18 ▶ Poet Laureate

39/19 ▶ George the Sixth

39/20 ▶ Monopoly

39/21 ▶ Nick Cotton

39/22 ▶ Abebe Bikila

39/23 ▶ The Folies Bergère

The target to beat the Chaser is 18

Final Chase Quiz 40

40/1 ▶ King Herod

40/2 ▶ Tomato

40/3 ▶ Stockholm

40/4 ▶ Wedding

40/5 ▶ Puff Daddy

40/6 ▶ Arabic

40/7 ▶ Brian Lara

40/8 ▶ Ten

40/9 ▶ Bristol

40/10 ▶ Jones

40/11 ▶ J R R Tolkien

40/12 ▶ *The Archers*

40/13 ▶ L S Lowry

40/14 ▶ The Human League

40/15 ▶ Skoda

40/16 ▶ *The Poseidon Adventure*

40/17 ▶ Salad

40/18 ▶ Livy

40/19 ▶ Heart

40/20 ▶ Richard

40/21 ▶ Australia

40/22 ▶ *Oliver!*

40/23 ▶ Germany

The target to beat the Chaser is 19

Acknowledgements

Octopus Publishing Group would like to thank *The Chase* production team and all at Potato: Bradley Walsh, Michael Kelpie, Martin Scott, Helen Tumbridge, Caroline Sale, Christina Clayton, the Chasers – Mark Labbett, Anne Hegerty, Shaun Wallace, Paul Sinha – and especially the question team – Luke Kelly, James Bovington, Mary Doyle, Rachel Armitage, Thomas Eaton, Liz Gore, Sean Carey, Stewart McCartney, Angus McDonald, Abby Brakewell and Olav Bjortomt.

Picture Credits

101 Seraphim Art/Shutterstock; 123 AldanNi/Shutterstock; 145 vectorOK/Shutterstock; 167 Glam/Shutterstock.

Additional Text: Justin Lewis
Editorial Director: Trevor Davies
Senior Editor: Leanne Bryan
Designer: Penny Stock
Cover Designers: Penny Stock and Jack Storey
Picture Researcher: Jennifer Veall
Production Controller: Sarah-Jayne Johnson